Waffles, Crêpes and Pancakes

Waffles, Crêpes and Pancakes

With delicious
toppings and fillings

Norma Miller

RIGHT WAY

Constable & Robinson Ltd
55-56 Russell Square
London WC1B 4HP

www.constablerobinson.com

First published in the UK by Right Way,
an imprint of Constable & Robinson, 2011

A copy of the British Library Cataloguing in Publication Data
is available from the British Library

ISBN: 978-0-7160-2283-1

Printed and bound in China

1 3 5 7 9 10 8 6 4 2

Contents

Acknowledgements

The recipes in the book were developed using
the Andrew James pancake maker and waffle makers:

Andrew James UK Ltd.
www.andrewjamesworlwide.com
Tel: 0844 335 8464

Introduction

I REMEMBER, AS A CHILD, eating hot pancakes sprinkled with sugar and a little lemon juice squeezed on top. What a treat. My memories are of something quite traditional, and waffles, crêpes and pancakes have a long history in many countries. They have long been a great stand-by of street vendors, a delicious and comforting treat on a cold, crisp day. But they are in no way old-fashioned. In fact, waffles, crêpes and pancakes are immensely popular these days, and very modern in the way they fit in with contemporary lifestyles.

They are so easy and simple to make, they are irresistible and such great fun they can bring a smile to your face. You can launch a waffle party or a pancake party with great panache by using some quick and straightforward cooking techniques in front of your friends, making for a nice bit of theatre and performance art.

Varied and versatile, waffles, crêpes and pancakes can be served on almost any occasion. The basic batter can be made from simple ingredients already in your kitchen – just flour, eggs and milk. Variation comes from the use of different types of flour and the addition of liquids and flavourings. The results can be as simple or as elaborate as you like, as adventurous or imaginative.

With worldwide ingredients to choose from, waffles, crêpes and pancakes can be sweet or savoury, rolled or folded, filled or topped (or both), thick or thin, or even misshapen; it doesn't matter at all. Throughout the book there are plenty of serving suggestions and hints and tips to go with the recipes, and the preparation and cooking processes for each recipe are simple, straightforward and easy to follow.

So don't delay. Set up a waffle party or a pancake party today.

Equipment

VERY FEW PIECES of equipment are needed to make successful waffles and pancakes. I have enjoyed developing and testing these recipes using an electric waffle maker which makes petal-shaped waffles and a Belgian waffle maker which makes oblong waffles. I made pancakes with both an electric crêpe maker as well as a heavy-based non-stick frying pan or griddle pan.

Waffle Makers

Waffle makers are hinged machines which open to reveal two hot plates incised to give a honey-comb pattern to the cooked batter. The heating plates are non-stick and usually don't need to be brushed with oil before cooking.

Before Using a Waffle Maker for the First Time

With a new machine it is usual to heat the machine without food inside (see manufacturer's instruction leaflet). This helps to seal the heating plates and remove any residue left by the manufacturing process and is carried out only once.

Open the waffle maker and brush the heating plates with a little oil or melted butter. Close the lid, switch on the power and a red light and a green light will glow. Turn the dial to 'Max' and the machine will warm up (4–5 minutes). The green light will go out when the correct temperature is reached. Initially there may be a little smoke and odour. Allow the machine to cool down and clean when cold (see opposite). You are now ready to make waffles.

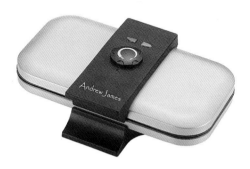

An electric Waffle Maker

An electric Belgian Waffle Maker

Crêpe Makers

Crêpe makers have a temperature-controlled 'TOP' plate on which the batter is spread. Make large pancakes covering the whole surface or three or four smaller pancakes.

An electric Crêpe Maker

Before Using a Crêpe Maker for the First Time

With a new machine it is usual to heat the machine without any food (see manufacturer's instruction leaflet). This helps to seal the heating plate and remove any residue left by the manufacturing process and is carried out only once. Brush the 'TOP' cooking plate with a little oil or melted butter. Switch on the power and a red light and a green light will glow. Turn the dial to 'Max' and the machine will warm up (4–5 minutes). The green light will go out when the correct temperature is reached. Initially there may be a little smoke and odour. Allow the machine to cool down and clean when cold (see below). You are now ready to make crêpes.

Care and Cleaning

- Read the 'important safety advice section' (see overleaf).
- Always unplug the machines before cleaning.
- Turn the switch knob to the 'Min' position and leave to cool completely.
- Clean any food sticking to the surfaces as soon as the machines are cold.
- *Waffle machine*: Clean the inner cooking surfaces with a damp cloth and a mild detergent. Wipe the surfaces dry with a soft cloth and wipe over the outside of the machine.

- *Crêpe machine*: Clean the 'TOP' cooking surface with a damp cloth and a mild detergent. Wipe the surfaces dry with a soft cloth and wipe over the outside of the machine.
- Do not get any water inside the machines. *Never submerge the machines in water.*
- Do not use any abrasive cleaners or scouring pads as these can scratch and damage the non-stick surfaces.

Important Safety Advice

Much of this advice is common sense when using any electrical kitchen appliance:

- Before using either an electric crêpe or waffle maker for the first time always read the manufacturer's instruction leaflets.
- Place the machines on a flat, stable, heat-proof surface and not near the edge of work surfaces or near a heat source.
- Keep the surrounding areas clear and free from clutter.
- Never kink or clamp the mains lead (power cord).
- The machines become extremely hot, so don't touch the 'TOP' plate of the crêpe maker or the 'Outer' or 'Inner' surfaces of the waffle makers as they will burn.
- Keep children and pets away from the machines when in use.
- When cooking pancakes, crêpes or waffles, never leave the machines unattended.
- *Important:* Once you have finished cooking your pancakes, crêpes or waffles, *always s*witch the machines off immediately. *Don't forget this. Damage could be caused to the machines if they are left switched on for a prolonged period of time.*
- Always unplug the machines before cleaning.
- Don't immerse the machines, power cord or electric plug in hot water or place in a dishwasher.
- Only use the machines indoors.
- If any faults occur with the machines, repairs must always be carried out by a qualified technician.

About the Recipes

- For convenience, the recipe ingredients are listed in the order in which they are used.
- Though the measurements are given in imperial as well as metric, UK readers will find the metric measures easier.
- When measuring volumes of liquid, US readers should follow the cup quantities, since UK (not US) pints are used in the recipes.
- You will find both the British and the American names for many common ingredients throughout the book.
- Mostly the recipes serve four or two people, but quantities can be doubled or more than doubled in most cases in order to feed a crowd.
- All spoon measures are level unless otherwise stated.
- The recipes are often adaptable, and you can easily substitute interchangeable ingredients as you wish.
- Where a recipe calls for boiling water, I have used a kettle and then added the boiling water to the recipe. This not only saves time but can save energy too.
- For the recipes cooked in an oven, the oven is pre-heated. If you have a fan oven, pre-heating may not be needed, so check your instruction book.

- If a recipe uses a microwave oven, then the recipes have been tested in one with a wattage of 700–800W.
- If you are preparing food for someone who has a food allergy, be sure to study the list of ingredients carefully.
- A few recipes contain fresh chillies. Do take care when preparing them and remember to wash your hands thoroughly afterwards. Better still, wear rubber gloves while handling them.
- One or two recipes contain raw or partly cooked eggs – please remember that it may be advisable to avoid eating these if you are pregnant, elderly, very young or sick.

About the Ingredients

A BASIC BATTER IS made from ingredients which are probably already in your kitchen: flour, eggs and milk. With just a few other ingredients you can make many different variations. I like to use a mixture of fresh seasonal produce, dry ingredients and canned or bottled foods, as well as some frozen items.

- In my kitchen I always have small jars of pastes that are so quick and convenient – garlic, pesto, ginger, curry and chilli. Bottles of soy sauce, brown sauce, as well as flavoured oils and vinegars are always on hand. I also keep a wide selection of spices and spice mixes, canned or bottled tomatoes, passata and a selection of canned beans.
- I prefer to use fresh herbs, if possible, and freeze any excess, finely chopped in ice-cube trays.
- Different types of flour will give added flavour and textures to the batter mix. Replace some of the plain flour with spelt, wholegrain, cornmeal or buckwheat.
- I also find it's useful, or rather essential, to keep a few tubs of sorbet and ice cream tucked away in the freezer to spoon onto hot pancakes or waffles.

- Other favourite ingredients are jars or bottles of clear honey and maple syrup for pouring and drizzling, conserves to spread and, of course, chocolate to grate and melt.
- Both liquid concentrated stock and vegetable bouillon powder are very useful as you can use as much or as little as you want.
- Salt is kept to a minimum. Instead I prefer to source good quality ingredients that have bags of flavour. Often just a handful of freshly chopped herbs is all you need to boost flavour. A little salt is included in the recipes, but use with discretion and omit if you prefer.
- I've mentioned this before, but if you are cooking for someone who has a food allergy be sure to study the list of ingredients carefully.

About the History

VERSIONS OF PANCAKES and waffles have been around for a few hundred years. Both use simple ingredients. Pancakes are cooked on a griddle over a hot fire. Waffles are made from a light batter cake and are cooked in a waffle iron or device to give their characteristic honey-comb shape.

Waffles were originally cooked in a long-handled patterned iron which went over the fire. The batter mix is baked between two hot plates with incised patterns. The word comes from the Dutch *wafel*.

There are many names and types of pancakes to be found around the world: French crêpes are thin pancakes and often have a sweet or savoury filling. The thicker American breakfast pancake is also called a hotcake, griddlecake or flapjack. Then there are traditional Hungarian *palacsinta*; *bao bing*, a Chinese thin pancake made with wheat flour and very hot water; *schmarren* – popular in Germany and Austria; thicker Scottish pancakes such as drop scones; *dosas* from India; Russian *blinis* and Danish *ebelskivers* – small sphere-shaped pancakes.

In the United Kingdom and elsewhere, pancakes are traditionally eaten on Shrove Tuesday, also popularly known as Pancake Day. The last day before Lent, it is a time of abstinence leading up to Easter. Pancakes are a simple way of using up the eggs, milk and butter before Lent begins.

1

The Basics

Hints and Tips for Good Results

The Batter

- Mix the batter ingredients whichever way you prefer: in a food processor, in a bowl with a hand-held stick-blender, vigorously shaken in a bottle-shaped lidded container, or just use a mixing bowl or jug and a coil or balloon whisk. This last method is the one I have used in the recipes as it quickly gives a smooth batter with little effort.
- For any batter containing seeds, nuts or chopped ingredients, either sweet or savoury, the batter will need a good stir before use. Otherwise, the last pancake or waffle you make will have all the bits.
- An equivalent amount of batter can make variable numbers of pancakes or waffles, depending on factors such as their size or thickness.
- Replacing a little of the milk with an extra egg or stirring in a little melted butter will give rich-tasting pancakes or waffles.
- Baking powder, whisked egg whites or yeast add lightness to the batter.
- The batter can thicken if left to stand for a while, or overnight. Just stir in a little extra milk or water until the consistency is what you want.
- The first pancake of each batch made is often not very successful, but no-one knows why.

Waffles

- Don't overfill waffle makers, otherwise when the machine is closed the mixture will overflow. Also, as the mixture begins to cook it will rise, especially if yeast, baking powder or whisked egg whites are in the batter.
- Any fresh herbs or nuts stirred into the batter mixtures should be chopped very finely, otherwise they may stick and burn in the waffle maker.

Freezing Waffles and Pancakes

- Purists will say that the best pancakes and waffles are straight from the pan and piping hot, and they probably are. But I find it is so useful to have pancakes or waffles readily available in the freezer, and I think they freeze very successfully. Interleave the waffles or pancakes with parchment paper and put into freezer bags.

Reheating or Keeping Waffles and Pancakes Warm

- Thaw and use pancakes and waffles the same day.
- Arrange the pancakes and waffles on a baking sheet, interleaving with parchment paper if they overlap. Cover with foil and heat in a medium-hot oven for a few minutes until heated through.
- Reheat thawed pancakes in the microwave by putting one to six on kitchen paper (paper towels) on a plate. Microwave for 10 seconds to one minute, turning the stack over halfway through the heating time. Stand for one minute before serving.
- Single waffles can be heated in a toaster (if suitable).

Basic Waffle Recipe

The butter can be replaced with a light oil.

Makes about 8–10 waffles

115 g / 4 oz / 1 cup plain (all-purpose) flour
1 tsp baking powder
Pinch of salt
3 tbsp caster sugar
2 medium eggs
2 tbsp melted butter
300 ml / ½ pint / 1¼ cups milk

1. Sift the flour, baking powder and salt into a bowl and stir in the sugar. Make a well in the centre, break in the eggs and pour in the melted butter. With a whisk, gently stir the flour mixture into the eggs, gradually adding enough of the milk to make a smooth batter the consistency of single (light) cream.
2. Preheat the waffle maker to 'Medium' heat.
3. When at temperature, open the machine and pour a small ladleful of batter into the compartments, taking care not to overfill.
4. Close the machine and cook for 4–6 minutes until golden brown.
5. Cook the remaining batter, making about 8–10 waffles in total, and serve warm.

Basic Pancake Recipe

For a sweet version stir in a tablespoon of caster sugar. An equivalent amount of batter can make variable numbers of pancakes, depending on factors such as their size and thickness.

Makes 8–10 pancakes measuring about 10 cm / 4 inches across

115 g / 4 oz / 1 cup plain (all-purpose) flour
Pinch of salt
2 medium eggs
300 ml / ½ pint / 1¼ cups milk
Oil or melted butter

1. Sift the flour into a bowl and add the salt. Make a well in the centre and break in the eggs. With a whisk, gently stir the flour into the eggs, gradually adding the milk to make a smooth batter the consistency of single (light) cream. If time allows, cover and leave to stand for about 15 minutes.
2. Lightly brush the crêpe maker or a non-stick frying pan with a little oil or melted butter. Preheat the crêpe maker to 'Medium', or put the non-stick frying pan over a medium heat.
3. When hot, pour in a small ladleful of batter and spread or swirl to give a thin layer. Cook gently for about 30–45 seconds on one side until the underside is golden brown. Using a flat spatula or palette knife carefully flip the pancake over and cook the second side for about 30 seconds. Lift out and keep warm.
4. Cook the remaining batter, making about 8–10 pancakes in total, and serve warm.

2
Quick and Easy Savoury Recipes

AT ANY TIME OF THE DAY, for a snack or a quick and easy-to-make light meal, savoury pancakes and waffles are the perfect choice. There are many enticing things you can do with them, using fresh vegetables and herbs, dried spices and other healthy ingredients, to create lots of exciting flavours. These waffles, pancakes, crêpes, galettes and hotcakes need no accompaniment. But if you do fancy something more, just add a little meat or fish, some salad or a helping of beans.

Herb and Yogurt Waffles

Mixed herbs give the waffles lots of flavour, perfect for serving with barbecued fish or shellfish. The number of waffles a recipe makes depends upon the waffle maker – oblong or petal-shaped waffles will be of different sizes.

Serves 4

Small handful of mixed herbs, such as dill, parsley, thyme
115 g / 4 oz / 1 cup plain (all-purpose) flour
1 tsp baking powder
Pinch of salt
2 medium eggs
2 tbsp melted butter
150 ml / ¼ pint / ²/₃ cup natural yogurt
150 ml / ¼ pint / ²/₃ cup milk

1. Pull the herb leaves from the stalks and very finely chop.
2. Sift the flour, baking powder and salt into a bowl. Make a well in the centre, break in the eggs and pour in the melted butter. With a whisk, gently stir the flour mixture into the eggs, gradually adding the yogurt and enough of the milk to make a smooth batter the consistency of double (heavy) cream. Stir in the chopped herbs.
3. Preheat the waffle maker to 'Medium' heat.
4. When at temperature, open the machine and pour a small ladleful of batter into the compartments, taking care not to overfill.
5. Close the machine and cook for 4–6 minutes until golden brown.
6. Cook the remaining batter and serve warm.

Cheese and Ham Breton Crêpes

French crêpes are very thin. There is quite a skill to spreading the batter as thin as it will go. A traditional filling of ham and cheese is perfect with this pancake.

Serves 4

Filling
100 g / 3½ oz Gruyère cheese
6 slices lean cooked ham

Crêpes
55 g / 2 oz / ½ cup buckwheat flour
55 g / 2 oz / ½ cup plain (all-purpose) flour
Pinch of salt
2 medium eggs
1 tbsp melted butter
300 ml / ½ pint / 1¼ cups milk
Oil or melted butter

1. Grate the cheese and cut the ham into thin strips.
2. In a large bowl, mix together the buckwheat flour, plain (all-purpose) flour and salt. Make a well in the centre, break in the eggs and pour in the melted butter. With a whisk, gently stir the flour into the eggs, gradually adding enough of the milk to make a smooth batter the consistency of single (light) cream. If time allows, cover and leave to stand for about 15–30 minutes.

3. Pour the batter into a jug.
4. Lightly brush the crêpe maker or a non-stick frying pan with a little oil or melted butter. Preheat the crêpe maker to 'Medium', or put the non-stick frying pan over a medium heat.
5. When hot, pour a small ladleful of batter and spread or swirl to give a thin layer. Cook gently for about 30–45 seconds on one side until the underside is golden brown. Using a flat spatula or palette knife, carefully flip the crêpe over and cook the second side for about 20 seconds.
6. Scatter some of the grated cheese and strips of ham over the crêpe. Cook for about 10 seconds for the cheese to begin to melt. Fold the crêpe in half over the filling and serve immediately.
7. Cook the remaining batter, making about 8 pancakes in total.

Bacon and Parsley Pancakes

Baking powder gives a rise to these pancakes, so they will be a little thicker than, say, the French crêpes. Make them the size you like and serve with lashings of brown sauce or tomato ketchup. Don't freeze.

Serves 4

6 smoked back bacon rashers (strips)
A few parsley sprigs
115 g / 4 oz / 1 cup plain (all-purpose) flour
1 tsp baking powder
Pinch of salt
2 medium eggs
300 ml / ½ pint / 1¼ cups milk
Oil or melted butter

1. With scissors, trim the rind from the bacon rashers (strips) and cut the bacon into small pieces. Finely chop the parsley sprigs (about 1 tbsp).
2. Heat a small frying pan, add the bacon pieces and, without adding any fat, cook quickly until just beginning to brown. Lift out of the pan and drain on kitchen paper (paper towels).
3. Sift the flour and baking powder into a bowl and add the salt. Make a well in the centre and break in the eggs. With a whisk, gently stir the flour into the eggs, gradually adding enough of the milk to make a smooth batter the consistency of single (light) cream. If time allows, cover and leave to stand for about 15 minutes.

4. Stir the bacon pieces and chopped parsley into the batter.
5. Lightly brush the crêpe maker or a non-stick frying pan with a little oil or melted butter. Preheat the crêpe maker to 'Medium', or put the non-stick frying pan over a medium heat.
6. When hot, pour a small ladleful of batter and spread or swirl to give a thin layer. Cook gently for about 30–45 seconds on one side until the underside is golden brown. Using a flat spatula or palette knife, carefully flip the pancake over and cook the second side for about 30 seconds. Lift out and keep warm.
7. Cook the remaining batter, stirring each time to mix the bacon in the batter, making about 8–10 pancakes in total, and serve warm.

Gluten-free Chilli and Walnut Waffles

It's always useful to have a few gluten-free recipes available. Reduce the chilli for less 'heat'.

Makes about 8–10 waffles

½ red chilli (see page 8)
8 walnut halves
55 g / 2 oz / ½ cup rice flour
55 g / 2 oz / ½ cup gluten-free flour
1 tsp gluten-free baking powder
Pinch of salt
2 medium eggs
2 tbsp melted butter
300 ml / ½ pint / 1¼ cups milk

1. Remove any stalk and seeds from the chilli and finely chop. Chop the walnuts.
2. Sift the rice flour, gluten-free flour, gluten-free baking powder and salt into a bowl. Make a well in the centre, break in the eggs and pour in the melted butter. With a whisk, gently stir the flour mixture into the eggs, gradually adding enough of the milk to make a smooth batter the consistency of double (heavy) cream. Stir in the chopped chilli and walnuts.
3. Preheat the waffle maker to 'Medium' heat.
4. When at temperature, open the machine and pour a small ladleful of batter into the compartments, taking care not to overfill.
5. Close the machine and cook for 4–6 minutes until golden brown.
6. Cook the remaining batter and serve warm.

Parmesan and Oregano Yeasted Waffles

These waffles have a slight yeasty flavour and a more open texture. You can make the batter the night before and put into the fridge overnight. Take out of the fridge for 30 minutes before using.

Serves 6

2 sprigs oregano
115 g / 4 oz / 1 cup plain (all-purpose) flour
Pinch of salt
¼ tsp fast-action dried yeast
2 medium eggs
2 tbsp melted butter
300 ml / ½ pint / 1¼ cups milk
40 g / 1½ oz grated Parmesan cheese

1. Pull the oregano leaves from the stalks and roughly chop.
2. Sift the flour and salt into a bowl. Stir in the fast-action dried yeast. Make a well in the centre, break in the eggs and pour in the melted butter. With a whisk, gently stir the flour mixture into the eggs, gradually adding enough of the milk to make a smooth batter the consistency of double (heavy) cream. Stir in the oregano leaves and Parmesan cheese.
3. Cover the bowl with oiled clear film (plastic wrap) and leave in a warm place until doubled in size, about 45 minutes to an hour. Before using, mix the batter and, if too thick, stir in a little milk.
4. Preheat the waffle maker to 'Medium' heat.
5. When at temperature, open the machine and pour a small ladleful of batter into the compartments, taking care not to overfill.
6. Close the machine and cook for 4–6 minutes until golden brown.
7. Cook the remaining batter and serve warm.

Pancake Stacks with Lemon and Chive

A pile of pancakes always looks spectacular.

Serves 4

Filling
Small bunch chives
1 lemon
55g / 2 oz / ¼ cup softened butter
Freshly milled salt and pepper

Pancakes
115 g / 4 oz / 1 cup plain (all-purpose) flour
1 tbsp wholemeal (whole-wheat) flour
Pinch of salt
3 medium eggs
300 ml / ½ pint / 1¼ cups milk
Oil or melted butter

1. With scissors, finely snip the chives. Finely grate the rind from half the lemon, cut in half and squeeze out the juice. In a small bowl, mix together the softened butter, chives, lemon rind and a little seasoning.
2. Sift the plain (all-purpose) flour and wholemeal (whole-wheat) flour with a pinch of salt into a bowl. Make a well in the centre and break in the eggs. With a whisk, gently stir the flour into the eggs, gradually adding enough of the milk to make a smooth batter the consistency of single (light) cream. If time allows, cover and leave to stand for about 30 minutes.

3. Lightly brush the crêpe maker or a non-stick frying pan with a little oil or melted butter. Preheat the crêpe maker to 'Medium', or put the non-stick frying pan over a medium heat.

4. When hot, pour a small ladleful of batter and spread or swirl to give a thin layer. Cook gently for about 30–45 seconds on one side until the underside is golden brown. Using a flat spatula or palette knife, carefully flip the pancake over and cook the second side for about 30 seconds. Lift out and keep hot.

5. Cook the remaining batter, making about 8–10 pancakes in total. Put a pancake on a plate and thinly spread with a little chive mixture. Sprinkle over a few drops of lemon juice and top with another pancake. Repeat until the pancakes are in a stack. Serve hot, cut into wedges.

Sesame Seed Pancakes with Watercress and Feta Cheese Salad

For any batter containing seeds, nuts or chopped ingredients, the batter will need a good stir before ladling into the pan, otherwise the last pancake will have all the bits. If you like a stronger cheese, use goat's cheese.

Serves 4

Filling
1 bunch watercress
6 cherry tomatoes
175 g / 6 oz feta cheese
1 tbsp olive oil
½ tsp mild mustard
Freshly milled salt and pepper

Pancakes
115 g / 4 oz / 1 cup plain (all-purpose) flour
Pinch of salt
2 medium eggs
300 ml / ½ pint / 1¼ cups milk
2 tbsp sesame seeds
Oil or melted butter

1. Pull the watercress leaves from the stalks. Quarter the tomatoes and cut the feta cheese into small cubes. Pour the oil into a bowl, stir in the mustard and season with salt and pepper. Add the watercress leaves, tomato wedges and the feta cheese. Gently fold the ingredients in the dressing.
2. Sift the flour into a bowl and add a pinch of salt. Make a well in the centre and break in the eggs. With a whisk, gently stir the flour into the eggs, gradually adding enough of the milk to make a smooth batter the consistency of single (light) cream. Stir in the sesame seeds and, if time allows, cover and leave to stand for about 15 minutes.
3. Lightly brush the crêpe maker or a non-stick frying pan with a little oil or melted butter. Preheat the crêpe maker to 'Medium', or put the non-stick frying pan over a medium heat.
4. When hot, stir the batter and pour a small ladleful of batter and spread or swirl to give a thin layer. Cook gently for about 30–45 seconds on one side until the underside is golden brown. Using a flat spatula or palette knife, carefully flip the pancake over and cook the second side for about 30 seconds. Lift out and keep warm.
5. Cook the remaining batter, making about 8 pancakes in total. Put some of the filling on one half of the pancake and fold the other half over. Serve immediately.

Sun-dried Tomato and Olive Waffles

If you don't like olives, replace with a few chopped walnuts or pecan nuts.

Serves 4

8 black pitted olives
1 piece of sun-dried tomato in oil (2 tbsp chopped)
115 g / 4 oz / 1 cup plain (all-purpose) flour
1 tsp baking powder
Pinch of salt
2 medium eggs
2 tbsp melted butter
300 ml / ½ pint / 1¼ cups milk

1. Halve the olives and thinly slice. Finely chop the sun-dried tomatoes.
2. Sift the flour, baking powder and salt into a bowl. Make a well in the centre, break in the eggs and pour in the melted butter. With a whisk, gently stir the flour mixture into the eggs, gradually adding enough of the milk to make a smooth batter the consistency of single (light) cream. Stir in the sliced olives and chopped sun-dried tomatoes.
3. Preheat the waffle maker to 'Medium' heat.
4. When at temperature, open the machine and pour a small ladleful of batter into the compartments, taking care not to overfill.
5. Close the machine and cook for 4–6 minutes until golden brown.
6. Cook the remaining batter, making about 8–10 waffles in total, and serve warm.

Potato Flour Waffles with Soured Cream

If potato flour isn't available, replace with wholemeal (whole-wheat). Great for breakfast with grilled (broiled) mushrooms.

Serves 4–6

55 g / 2 oz / ½ cup plain (all-purpose) flour
55 g / 2 oz / ½ cup potato flour
1½ tsp baking powder
Pinch of ground nutmeg
Pinch of salt
2 medium eggs
2 tbsp melted butter
2 tbsp soured cream
300 ml / ½ pint / 1¼ cups milk less 2 tbsp

1. Sift the plain (all-purpose) flour, potato flour, baking powder, nutmeg and salt into a bowl. Make a well in the centre, break in the eggs and pour in the melted butter. With a whisk, gently stir the flour mixture into the eggs, gradually adding the soured cream and enough of the milk to make a smooth batter the consistency of single (light) cream.
2. Preheat the waffle maker to 'Medium' heat.
3. When at temperature, open the machine and pour a small ladleful of batter into the compartments, taking care not to overfill.
4. Close the machine and cook for 4–6 minutes until golden brown.
5. Cook the remaining batter and serve warm.

Herb Crêpes with Scrambled Eggs and Mushrooms

If you're cooking these for breakfast or brunch, prepare the batter the evening before. Cover and put in the fridge. Take the batter out 30 minutes before use. It may have thickened up, so just add a little milk or water.

Serves 2–4

Crêpes
115 g / 4 oz / 1 cup buckwheat flour
Pinch of salt
2 tbsp freeze-dried chervil or parsley
2 tbsp melted butter
2 medium eggs
300 ml / ½ pint / 1¼ cups milk
Oil or melted butter

Filling
1 handful of button mushrooms
2 tsp butter
5 medium eggs
Freshly milled black pepper

1. Sift the flour into a bowl and add the salt. Make a well in the centre, add the chervil or parsley, melted butter, and break in the eggs. With a whisk, gently stir the flour into the eggs, gradually adding the milk to make a smooth batter the consistency of single (light) cream. If time allows, cover and leave to stand for about 15 minutes.
2. Lightly brush the crêpe maker or a large non-stick frying pan with a little oil or melted butter. Preheat the crêpe maker to 'Medium', or put the non-stick frying pan over a medium heat.

3. When hot, pour a small ladleful of batter and spread or swirl to give a thin layer. Cook gently for about 30–45 seconds on one side until the underside is golden brown. Using a flat spatula or palette knife, carefully flip the crêpe over and cook the second side for about 30 seconds. Lift out and keep warm.
4. Cook the remaining batter, making about 4 large or 8 medium-sized crêpes in total and keep warm.
5. Prepare the filling as the crêpes cook. Thinly slice the mushrooms. Heat the butter in a small non-stick pan and cook the mushrooms until golden.
6. Break the eggs into a bowl, season with pepper and beat lightly with a fork. Pour over the hot mushrooms, and, stirring continuously, gently cook until almost set.
7. Spoon onto the crêpes and serve immediately.

American Hotcakes with Chilli Sausages

Perfect combination, light fluffy hotcakes with hot sticky sausages.

Serves 4

Hotcakes
115 g / 4 oz / 1 cup plain (all-purpose) flour
2 tsp baking powder
Pinch of salt
2 medium eggs
150 ml / ¼ pint / $^2/_3$ cup natural yogurt
150 ml / ¼ pint / $^2/_3$ cup milk
Oil or melted butter

Topping
8 butchers sausages, choose your favourite
3 tbsp sweet chilli sauce
1 tbsp tomato ketchup

1. Sift the flour and baking powder into a bowl and add the salt. Make a well in the centre and break in the eggs. With a whisk, gently stir the flour into the eggs, gradually adding the yogurt and enough of the milk to make a smooth batter the consistency of double (heavy) cream. If time allows, cover and leave to stand for about 15 minutes.

2. Cook the sausages as you are making the hotcakes. In a small bowl mix together the sweet chilli sauce and tomato ketchup. Arrange the sausages on a grill (broiling) pan and brush with the sauce. Grill (broil) under a medium heat until cooked through, turning and brushing with the sauce.

3. Lightly brush the crêpe maker or a non-stick frying pan with a little oil or melted butter. Preheat the crêpe maker to 'Medium', or put the non-stick frying pan over a medium heat.

4. When hot, pour a small ladleful of batter and spread to give a small hotcake. Cook gently for about 30–45 seconds on one side until the underside is golden brown. Using a flat spatula or palette knife, carefully flip the hotcake over and cook the second side for about 30–45 seconds. Lift out and keep warm.

5. Cook the remaining batter, and serve with the hot sticky sausages.

Malted Waffles with Celery Seeds

Malt and celery seeds give an earthy, full-bodied flavour.

Serves 4–6

115 g / 4 oz / 1 cup plain (all-purpose) flour
1 tsp baking powder
Pinch of salt
1 tsp celery seeds
2 medium eggs
2 tbsp melted butter
2 tsp malt extract
300 ml / ½ pint / 1¼ cups milk

1. Sift the flour, baking powder and salt into a bowl and stir in the celery seeds. Make a well in the centre, break in the eggs and pour in the melted butter and malt extract. With a whisk, gently stir the flour mixture into the eggs, gradually adding enough of the milk to make a smooth batter the consistency of single (light) cream.
2. Preheat the waffle maker to 'Medium' heat.
3. When at temperature, open the machine and pour a small ladleful of batter into the compartments, taking care not to overfill.
4. Close the machine and cook for 4–6 minutes until golden brown.
5. Cook the remaining batter, making about 8–10 waffles in total, and serve warm.

Buckwheat Crêpes with Prawns (Shrimps)

Buttermilk adds a slightly sour flavour to the batter. If not available, add a few drops of lemon juice to ordinary milk to sour it just a little. Make small pancakes the size of a small teacup and serve with pickle or relish.

Serves 4

200 g / 7 oz cooked, peeled prawns (shrimps), thawed if frozen
115 g / 4 oz / 1 cup buckwheat flour
Freshly milled salt and pepper
3 medium eggs
300 ml / ½ pint / 1¼ cups buttermilk or milk
1 tsp lemon juice
2 tbsp melted butter
Oil or melted butter

1. Cut each prawn (shrimp) into three or four. Drain on kitchen paper (paper towels).
2. Sift the flour into a bowl and add a little salt and pepper. Make a well in the centre and break in the eggs. With a whisk, gently stir the flour into the eggs, gradually adding enough of the buttermilk or milk to make a smooth batter the consistency of single (light) cream. Stir in the lemon juice and melted butter. If time allows, cover and leave to stand for about 15 minutes.
3. Lightly brush the crêpe maker or a non-stick frying pan with a little oil or melted butter. Preheat the crêpe maker to 'Medium', or put the non-stick frying pan over a medium heat.
4. When hot, pour a small ladleful of batter and spread or swirl to give a thin layer the size of a small teacup. As the crêpe cooks put a few pieces of prawn (shrimp) onto the crêpe and gently push into the batter. Cook gently for about 30–45 seconds on one side until the underside is golden brown. Using a flat spatula or palette knife, carefully flip the crêpe over and cook the second side for about 30 seconds. Lift out and keep warm.
5. Cook the remaining batter and serve warm.

Pine Nut, Parsley and Basil Waffles

The flavours of pesto in a waffle.

Serves 4–6

Small handful of parsley leaves
Small handful of basil leaves
55 g / 2 oz pine nuts
115 g / 4 oz / 1 cup plain (all-purpose) flour
1 tsp baking powder
Pinch of salt
2 medium eggs
2 tbsp melted butter
300 ml / ½ pint / 1¼ cups milk

1. Finely chop the parsley, basil leaves and pine nuts.
2. Sift the flour, baking powder and salt into a bowl. Make a well in the centre, break in the eggs and pour in the melted butter. With a whisk, gently stir the flour mixture into the eggs, gradually adding enough of the milk to make a smooth batter the consistency of single (light) cream. Stir in the chopped parsley, basil and pine nuts.
3. Preheat the waffle maker to 'Medium' heat.
4. When at temperature, open the machine and pour a small ladleful of batter into the compartments, taking care not to overfill.
5. Close the machine and cook for 4–6 minutes until golden brown.
6. Cook the remaining batter, making about 8–10 waffles in total, and serve warm.

Onion and Mustard Galettes

Spread with smooth chicken liver pâté, then roll up the galette, slice and serve with salad and a cucumber relish.

Serves 4

3 spring onions
115 g / 4 oz / 1 cup buckwheat flour
Pinch of salt
2 medium eggs
300 ml / ½ pint / 1¼ cups milk
1 tsp mild mustard
Oil or melted butter

1. Finely chop the spring onions.
2. Sift the flour into a bowl and add the salt. Make a well in the centre and break in the eggs. With a whisk, gently stir the flour into the eggs, gradually adding the milk to make a smooth batter the consistency of single (light) cream. Stir in the mustard and chopped spring onions. If time allows, cover and leave to stand for about 15 minutes.
3. Lightly brush the crêpe maker or a non-stick frying pan with a little oil or melted butter. Preheat the crêpe maker to 'Medium', or put the non-stick frying pan over a medium heat.
4. When hot, pour a small ladleful of batter and spread or swirl to give a thin layer. Cook gently for about 30–45 seconds on one side until the underside is golden brown. Using a flat spatula or palette knife, carefully flip the galette over and cook the second side for about 30 seconds. Lift out and keep warm.
5. Cook the remaining batter and serve warm.

Spiced Waffles with Cucumber and Coriander (Cilantro) Topping

A hint of curry flavours with a cooling topping.

Serves 4–6

Topping
1 medium-sized red onion
½ cucumber
Small bunch of coriander (cilantro)
300 ml / ½ pint / 1¼ cups thick natural yogurt
Freshly milled salt and black pepper

Waffles
115 g / 4 oz / 1 cup cornmeal flour
1 tsp baking powder
½ tsp mild curry powder
½ tsp ground coriander
Pinch of salt
2 medium eggs
2 tbsp olive oil
300 ml / ½ pint / 1¼ cups milk

1. Cut the onion in half and very finely shred. Slice the cucumber in half and scrape out and discard the seeds. Finely chop the cucumber with the coriander (cilantro) leaves.
2. Pour the yogurt into a bowl and stir in the shredded onion, chopped cucumber and coriander (cilantro). Mix and stir in a little seasoning to taste. Cover and chill until the waffles are made.

3. Sift the flour, baking powder, mild curry powder, ground coriander and salt into a bowl. Make a well in the centre, break in the eggs and pour in the oil. With a whisk, gently stir the flour mixture into the eggs, gradually adding enough of the milk to make a smooth batter the consistency of single (light) cream.
4. Preheat the waffle maker to 'Medium' heat.
5. When at temperature, open the machine and pour a small ladleful of batter into the compartments, taking care not to overfill.
6. Close the machine and cook for 4–6 minutes until golden brown and crisp.
7. Cook the remaining batter and serve warm with the yogurt topping.

Rice Pancakes with Sweet and Sour Vegetables

For speed, I've used a ready-made sauce in the filling. Choose a good quality one.

Serves 4–6

Filling
3 spring onions (scallions)
2 courgettes (zucchini)
1 carrot
Large handful of mange-touts
1 tbsp oil
Large handful of small spinach leaves
300 ml / ½ pint / 1¼ cups sweet and sour sauce

Pancakes
115 g / 4 oz / 1 cup rice flour
Pinch of salt
2 medium eggs
300 ml / ½ pint / 1¼ cups milk
Oil or melted butter

1. Thinly slice the spring onions (scallions) and cut the courgettes (zucchini) and carrot into thin strips. Cut each mange-tout into three lengthways.
2. Sift the flour into a bowl and add the salt. Make a well in the centre and break in the eggs. With a whisk, gently stir the flour into the eggs, gradually adding enough of the milk to make a smooth batter the consistency of single (light) cream. If time allows, cover and leave to stand for about 15 minutes.
3. Lightly brush the crêpe maker or a non-stick frying pan with a little oil or melted butter. Preheat the crêpe maker to 'Medium', or put the non-stick frying pan over a medium heat.
4. When hot, pour a small ladleful of batter and spread or swirl to give a thin layer. Cook gently for about 30–45 seconds on one side until the underside is golden brown. Using a flat spatula or palette knife, carefully flip the pancake over and cook the second side for about 30 seconds. Lift out and keep warm.
5. Cook the remaining batter and serve warm.
6. Cook the filling while the pancakes are being made. Heat the oil in a large pan and stir-fry the sliced spring onions (scallions), courgette (zucchini) and carrot for 3–4 minutes. Stir in the spinach leaves and sliced mange-touts and cook for a further minute.
7. Pour over the sauce, bring to the boil and cook until piping hot.
8. Spoon the sauce and vegetables onto the warm pancakes and roll or fold over.

Cheese and Soured Cream Waffles

Use a good strong cheese to give lots of flavour and serve with chutney and salad.

Serves 4–6

85 g / 3 oz mature Cheddar cheese
115 g / 4 oz / 1 cup plain (all-purpose) flour
1 tsp baking powder
¼ tsp paprika pepper
Freshly milled salt
3 medium eggs
2 tbsp melted butter
4 tbsp soured cream
300 ml / ½ pint / 1¼ cups milk

1. Finely grate the cheese. Sift the flour, baking powder, paprika pepper and salt into a bowl. Make a well in the centre, break in the eggs and pour in the melted butter. With a whisk, gently stir the flour mixture into the eggs, gradually adding the soured cream and enough of the milk to make a smooth batter the consistency of double (heavy) cream. Stir in the grated cheese.
2. Preheat the waffle maker to 'Medium' heat.
3. When at temperature, open the machine and pour a small ladleful of batter into the compartments, taking care not to overfill.
4. Close the machine and cook for 4–6 minutes until golden brown and crisp.
5. Cook the remaining batter, and serve warm.

3
Quick and Easy Sweet Recipes

LIFE CAN BE SO SWEET; pancakes to gobble up or delicately nibble on at your pleasure, and waffles to woof down whenever you want them. These sweet treats are so good for sharing with friends and family, or you may prefer to eat them by yourself (a guilty secret).

Cinnamon Orange Waffles or Cherry Hotcakes go really well on the breakfast table, Choc-Chip Waffles with Orange Drizzle would brighten up any afternoon, and the Lemon Pancake Layer with Berries looks amazing whenever you want to put on a bit of a show.

Don't forget, you can switch the toppings and fillings around with many of these recipes to come up with your favourite combinations.

Ricotta and Sultana Pancakes

Ricotta is a soft fresh cheese with a sweet tang. It adds a rich flavour to these small thick pancakes. Spread with unsalted butter or drizzle with maple syrup.

Serves 4–6

175 g / 6 oz / 1½ cups self-raising (self-rising) flour
2 tbsp caster sugar
2 medium eggs
2 tbsp melted butter
140 g / 5 oz ricotta cheese
300 ml / ½ pint / 1¼ cups milk
4 tbsp small sultanas
Oil or melted butter

1. Sift the flour into a bowl and stir in the sugar. Make a well in the centre and break in the eggs, pour in the melted butter and add the ricotta cheese. With a whisk, gently stir the flour into the eggs, gradually adding enough of the milk to make a smooth batter the consistency of single (light) cream. Stir in the sultanas. If time allows, cover and leave to stand for 15–30 minutes.
2. Lightly brush the crêpe maker or a non-stick frying pan with a little oil or melted butter. Preheat the crêpe maker to 'Medium', or put the non-stick frying pan over a medium heat.
3. When hot, pour a small ladleful of batter and spread or swirl to give a small pancake. Cook gently for about 30–45 seconds on one side until the underside is golden brown. Using a flat spatula or palette knife, carefully flip the pancake over and cook the second side for about 30 seconds. Lift out and keep warm.
4. Cook the remaining batter and serve warm.

Lemon Pancake Layer with Berries

Use your favourite selection of fruit in the filling, or spread the pancakes with fruit conserve mixed with some crème fraîche. Serve with scoops of vanilla ice cream, yogurt or cream.

Serves 4–6

Filling
1 lemon
350 g / 12 oz mixed frozen berries, such as raspberries, strawberries and blueberries
2 tbsp light brown sugar

Pancakes
115 g / 4 oz / 1 cup plain (all-purpose) flour
Pinch of salt
1 tbsp light brown sugar
2 medium eggs
300 ml / ½ pint / 1¼ cups milk
Oil or melted butter
Icing sugar, to dust

1. Finely grate the rind from the lemon (reserving 1 tbsp for the batter), cut in half and squeeze out the juice. Put the frozen fruits into a pan, add 2 tbsp cold water, the sugar, lemon juice and the remaining lemon rind. Cook over a gentle heat until the fruits start to collapse and the liquid has reduced. Remove from the heat and crush the fruits with a fork or potato masher.

2. Sift the flour into a bowl and add the salt, sugar and 1 tbsp of the lemon rind. Make a well in the centre and break in the eggs. With a whisk, gently stir the flour into the eggs, gradually adding enough of the milk to make a smooth batter the consistency of single (light) cream. If time allows, cover and leave to stand for about 30 minutes.
3. Lightly brush the crêpe maker or a non-stick frying pan with a little oil or melted butter. Preheat the crêpe maker to 'Medium', or put the non-stick frying pan over a medium heat.
4. When hot, pour a small ladleful of batter and spread or swirl to give a thin layer. Cook gently for about 30–45 seconds on one side until the underside is golden brown. Using a flat spatula or palette knife, carefully flip the pancake over and cook the second side for about 30 seconds. Lift out and keep hot.
5. Cook the remaining batter, making about 8–10 pancakes in total.
6. Put a pancake onto a plate and spoon over some of the fruit mixture. Spread almost to the edges and top with another pancake. Repeat until all the pancakes are used. To serve, dust with icing sugar and cut into wedges.

Vanilla Waffles with Raspberries and Hazelnut Cream

(as shown on the front cover)

A simple recipe with some classic, subtle flavours.

Serves 4–6

Topping
350 g / 12 oz raspberries, thawed if frozen
55 g / 2 oz toasted hazelnuts
300 ml / ½ pint / generous 1¼ cups double (heavy) cream
A drop of vanilla extract
A few mint leaves

Waffles
115 g / 4 oz / 1 cup plain (all-purpose) flour
1 tsp baking powder
Pinch of salt
3 tbsp caster sugar
2 medium eggs
2 tbsp melted butter
A few drops of vanilla extract
300 ml / ½ pint / 1¼ cups milk

1. If fresh, remove any stalks from the raspberries and chill. Finely chop the hazelnuts and lightly whip the cream. Stir half of the chopped nuts into the cream with the drop of vanilla extract and chill. Reserve the remaining nuts for decoration.

2. Sift the flour, baking powder and salt into a bowl and stir in the sugar. Make a well in the centre, break in the eggs and pour in the melted butter and a few drops of vanilla extract. With a whisk, gently stir the flour mixture into the eggs, gradually adding enough of the milk to make a smooth batter the consistency of double (heavy) cream.
3. Preheat the waffle maker to 'Medium' heat.
4. When at temperature, open the machine and pour a small ladleful of batter into the compartments, taking care not to overfill.
5. Close the machine and cook for 4–6 minutes until golden brown. Keep warm.
6. Cook the remaining batter. Serve the warm waffles topped with a spoonful of hazelnut cream, a few raspberries and a sprinkling of chopped nuts, and garnished with a mint leaf.

Breton Crêpes with Cinnamon Honey Butter

French crêpes are very thin and delicate. Keep any left-over cinnamon butter in the fridge.

Serves 4–6

Topping
6 tbsp clear honey
2 tbsp unsalted soft butter
2 tsp ground cinnamon

Crêpes
55 g / 2 oz / ½ cup buckwheat flour
55 g / 2 oz / ½ cup plain (all-purpose) flour
Pinch of salt
1 tbsp caster sugar
1 tbsp grated lemon rind
2 medium eggs
1 tbsp melted butter
300 ml / ½ pint / 1¼ cups milk
Oil or melted butter

1. Pour the honey into a small bowl and add the butter and cinnamon. Beat with a spoon until thoroughly mixed, light and airy.
2. Sift the flours and salt into a bowl and add the sugar and lemon rind. Make a well in the centre, break in the eggs and pour in the melted butter. With a whisk, gently stir the flour into the eggs, gradually adding enough of the milk to make a smooth batter the consistency of single (light) cream. If time allows, cover and leave to stand for about 30 minutes.

3. Lightly brush the crêpe maker or a non-stick frying pan with a little oil or melted butter. Preheat the crêpe maker to 'Medium', or put the non-stick frying pan over a medium heat.
4. When hot, pour a small ladleful of batter and spread or swirl to give a thin layer. Cook gently for about 30–45 seconds on one side until the underside is golden brown. Using a flat spatula or palette knife, carefully flip the crêpe over and cook the second side for about 30 seconds. Lift out and keep warm.
5. Cook the remaining batter and keep warm.
6. Spread the crêpes with a little cinnamon honey butter, fold into quarters and eat immediately.

Waffles with Melon, Pomegranate and Mint

Fruit salad with a little brandy, but if you don't want the alcohol, just replace with more orange juice.

Serves 4–6

Topping
½ ripe cantaloupe melon
1 pomegranate
6 mint leaves
2 tbsp brandy, optional
2 tbsp orange juice
1 tbsp caster sugar

Waffles
115 g / 4 oz / 1 cup plain (all-purpose) flour
1 tsp baking powder
Pinch of ground ginger
Pinch of salt
3 tbsp caster sugar
2 medium eggs
2 tbsp melted butter
300 ml / ½ pint / 1¼ cups milk

1. Cut the melon into three slices. Scoop out and discard the seeds. Cut the flesh from the rind and cut into slices. Cut the pomegranate in half and scoop out the seeds. Tear the mint leaves into small pieces.
2. Put the brandy (if using), orange juice and sugar into a bowl. Stir in the melon slices, pomegranate seeds and torn mint. Cover and leave for the flavours to infuse.

3. Sift the flour, baking powder, ground ginger and salt into a bowl and stir in the sugar. Make a well in the centre, break in the eggs and pour in the melted butter. With a whisk, gently stir the flour mixture into the eggs, gradually adding enough of the milk to make a smooth batter the consistency of double (heavy) cream.
4. Preheat the waffle maker to 'Medium' heat.
5. When at temperature, open the machine and pour a small ladleful of batter into the compartments, taking care not to overfill.
6. Close the machine and cook for 4–6 minutes until golden brown and crisp.
7. Cook the remaining batter and keep warm.
8. Serve the warm waffles topped with the brandied fruits.

Yeasted Pancakes with Pecan Fudge Sauce

These pancakes have a slight yeasty flavour and a more open texture. You can make the batter the night before and put it into the fridge overnight. If you do this, take the batter out of the fridge 30 minutes before use.

Serves 4–6

Fudge Sauce
70 g / 2½ oz pecan nuts
1 tbsp cornflour (cornstarch)
2 tbsp butter
3 tbsp soft brown sugar
1 small 175 g / 6 oz can evaporated milk

Pancakes
115 g / 4 oz / 1 cup plain (all-purpose) flour
Pinch of salt
2 tbsp soft brown sugar
½ tsp fast-action dried yeast
2 medium eggs
2 tbsp melted butter
300 ml / ½ pint / 1¼ cups milk
Oil or melted butter

1. Chop the pecan nuts. Blend the cornflour (cornstarch) in a cup with 2 tbsp cold water. Put the butter and sugar into a pan over a low heat and stir until the sugar has dissolved. Bring to the boil and stir in the evaporated milk and the blended cornflour (cornstarch). Cook for a minute or two until thick and smooth. Stir in the chopped pecan nuts.

2. Sift the flour and salt into a bowl and add the sugar. Stir in the yeast. Make a well in the centre and break in the eggs and pour in the melted butter. With a whisk, gently stir the flour into the eggs, gradually adding enough of the milk to make a smooth batter the consistency of single (light) cream. Cover the bowl with oiled clear film (plastic wrap) and leave in a warm place until doubled in size, about 45 minutes to an hour. Before using, mix the batter and, if too thick, stir in a little milk.

3. Lightly brush the crêpe maker or a non-stick frying pan with a little oil or melted butter. Preheat the crêpe maker to 'Medium', or put the non-stick frying pan over a medium heat.

4. When hot, pour in a small ladleful of batter and spread out to the size of a small teacup. Cook gently for about 30–45 seconds on one side until the underside is golden brown. Using a flat spatula or palette knife, carefully flip the pancake over and cook the second side for about 30 seconds. Lift out and keep warm.

5. Cook the remaining batter and keep warm. Heat the sauce and spoon over the hot pancakes.

Choc-Chip Waffles with Orange Drizzle

The combination of orange and mint flavours is not to everyone's taste, but I love it. So I sometimes replace the plain choc-chips with coarsely grated mint chocolate. Serve with ice cream.

Serves 4–6

Orange Drizzle
1 orange
2 tbsp golden syrup or pancake syrup

Waffles
55 g / 2 oz / ½ cup plain (all-purpose) flour
55 g / 2 oz / ½ cup buckwheat flour
1 tsp baking powder
Pinch of salt
2 tbsp caster sugar
2 medium eggs
2 tbsp melted butter
300 ml / ½ pint / 1¼ cups milk
60 g / 2¼ oz plain chocolate-chips

1. Finely grate the rind from half the orange. Cut in half and squeeze out the juice. Put the golden syrup or pancake syrup, orange rind, juice and orange into a microwave bowl and cook on a low power for a few seconds until the orange rind is soft.

2. Sift the flours, baking powder and salt into a bowl and stir in the sugar. Make a well in the centre, break in the eggs and pour in the melted butter. With a whisk, gently stir the flour mixture into the eggs, gradually adding enough of the milk to make a smooth batter the consistency of single (light) cream. Stir in the choc-chips.
3. Preheat the waffle maker to 'Medium' heat.
4. When at temperature, open the machine and pour a small ladleful of batter into the compartments, taking care not to overfill.
5. Close the machine and cook for 4–6 minutes until golden brown.
6. Cook the remaining batter and keep warm. Serve the waffles with the orange drizzle.

Cranberry Waffles

You can use any dried fruit in this recipe. Just chop the fruit into small pieces, otherwise it may stick in the machines.

Serves 4–6

60 g / 2¼ oz dried cranberries
115 g / 4 oz / 1 cup plain (all-purpose) flour
1 tsp baking powder
Pinch of salt
3 tbsp caster sugar
1 tsp grated lemon rind
2 medium eggs
2 tbsp melted butter
300 ml / ½ pint / 1¼ cups milk
Icing sugar, to dust

1. Roughly chop the cranberries.
2. Sift the flour, baking powder and salt into a bowl and stir in the sugar and lemon rind. Make a well in the centre, break in the eggs and pour in the melted butter. With a whisk, gently stir the flour mixture into the eggs, gradually adding enough of the milk to make a smooth batter the consistency of single (light) cream. Stir in the chopped cranberries.
3. Preheat the waffle maker to 'Medium' heat.
4. When at temperature, open the machine and pour a small ladleful of batter into the compartments, taking care not to overfill.
5. Close the machine and cook for 4–6 minutes until golden brown.
6. Cook the remaining batter, and serve warm, dusted with icing sugar.

Gluten-free Chocolate Pancakes

Anything made with chocolate looks impressive, even though these pancakes are so simple to make. Serve with vanilla ice cream and blueberries.

Serves 4–6

55 g / 2 oz / ½ cup rice flour
55 g / 2 oz / ½ cup gluten-free flour
½ tsp gluten-free baking powder
Pinch of salt
50 g / 1¾ oz grated dark or milk chocolate
2 medium eggs
2 tbsp melted butter
300 ml / ½ pint / 1¼ cups milk
Oil or melted butter

1. Sift the rice flour, gluten-free flour, gluten-free baking powder and salt into a bowl and add the grated chocolate. Make a well in the centre, break in the eggs and pour in the melted butter. With a whisk, gently stir the flour mixture into the eggs, gradually adding enough of the milk to make a smooth batter the consistency of single (light) cream.
2. Lightly brush the crêpe maker or a non-stick frying pan with a little oil or melted butter. Preheat the crêpe maker to 'Medium', or put the non-stick frying pan over a medium heat.
3. When hot, pour in a small ladleful of batter and spread or swirl to give a thin layer. Cook gently for about 30–45 seconds on one side until the underside is golden brown. Using a flat spatula or palette knife, carefully flip the pancake over and cook the second side for about 30 seconds. Lift out and keep warm.
4. Cook the remaining batter and serve warm.

Muesli (Granola) Waffles

Breakfast in a waffle. If you like muesli (granola), you'll love these. They'll taste slightly different with every muesli mix. Serve with fresh fruit and yogurt.

Serves 4–6

55 g / 2 oz muesli (granola)
55 g / 2 oz / ½ cup plain (all-purpose) flour
1 tsp baking powder
Pinch of salt
2 tbsp light brown sugar
2 medium eggs
2 tbsp melted butter
300 ml / ½ pint / 1¼ cups milk

1. Put the muesli (granola), flour, baking powder and salt into a bowl and stir in the sugar. Make a well in the centre, break in the eggs and pour in the melted butter. With a whisk, gently stir the flour mixture into the eggs, gradually adding enough of the milk to make a smooth batter the consistency of single (light) cream.
2. Preheat the waffle maker to 'Medium' heat.
3. When at temperature, open the machine and pour a small ladleful of batter into the compartments, taking care not to overfill.
4. Close the machine and cook for 4–6 minutes until golden brown.
5. Cook the remaining batter, and serve warm.

Coffee Crêpes

Fold the warm crêpes into quarters and serve with cream or yogurt to pour over.

Serves 4–6

115 g / 4 oz / 1 cup buckwheat flour
Pinch of salt
1 tbsp caster sugar
1 tbsp grated orange rind
2 medium eggs
1 tbsp melted butter
3 tbsp made espresso coffee
300 ml / ½ pint / 1¼ cups milk, less 3 tbsp
Oil or melted butter

1. Sift the flour and salt into a bowl, add the sugar and orange rind. Make a well in the centre, break in the eggs and pour in the melted butter. With a whisk, gently stir the flour into the eggs, gradually adding the coffee and enough of the milk to make a smooth batter the consistency of single (light) cream. If time allows, cover and leave to stand for about 30 minutes.
2. Lightly brush the crêpe maker or a non-stick frying pan with a little oil or melted butter. Preheat the crêpe maker to 'Medium', or put a non-stick frying pan over a medium heat.
3. When hot, pour a small ladleful of batter and spread or swirl to give a thin layer. Cook gently for about 30–45 seconds on one side until the underside is golden brown. Using a flat spatula or palette knife, carefully flip the crêpe over and cook the second side for about 30 seconds. Lift out and keep warm.
4. Cook the remaining batter and serve warm.

Waffles with Rose Water Syrup, Dried Fruits and Pistachio Nuts

Rose water gives a lovely exotic taste and fragrance to the syrup.

Serves 4–6

Syrup

4 tbsp golden syrup, or use pancake syrup
Small handful of raisins
Small handful of sultanas
Small handful of chopped pistachio nuts
Rose water, to taste

Waffles

3 medium eggs
115 g / 4 oz / 1 cup plain (all-purpose) flour
1 tsp baking powder
Pinch of salt
3 tbsp caster sugar
2 tsp rose water
2 tbsp melted butter
300 ml / ½ pint / 1¼ cups milk
Icing sugar, to dust

1. Spoon the syrup into a pan and stir in the raisins, sultanas, pistachio nuts and 4 tbsp cold water. Heat, and bring to the boil. Cook for 2–3 minutes. Leave to cool and stir in rose water, to taste.
2. Separate the eggs and put the whites into a grease-free bowl. Whisk the egg-whites until like soft peaks.

3. Sift the flour, baking powder and salt into a bowl and stir in the sugar. Make a well in the centre, add the egg yolks and rose water, and pour in the melted butter. With a whisk, gently stir the flour mixture into the egg yolks, gradually adding enough of the milk to make a smooth batter the consistency of double (heavy) cream.
4. Tip the whisked egg whites into the bowl of batter and with a spoon carefully fold in.
5. Preheat the waffle maker to 'Medium' heat.
6. When at temperature, open the machine and pour a small ladleful of batter into the compartments, taking care not to overfill.
7. Close the machine and cook for 4–6 minutes until golden brown.
8. Cook the remaining batter and keep warm.
9. Dust the warm waffles with icing sugar and serve with the syrup.

Rum and Coconut Galettes

Coconut adds lots of flavour and crunch to these galettes, and the rum seems to complement the tastes.

Serves 4–6

115 g / 4 oz / 1 cup buckwheat flour
1 tsp ground ginger
Pinch of salt
2 medium eggs
2 tbsp melted butter
1 tbsp rum, optional
300 ml / ½ pint / 1¼ cups milk, less 1 tbsp
4 tbsp desiccated coconut
Oil or melted butter

1. Sift the flour, ground ginger and salt into a bowl. Make a well in the centre, break in the eggs and pour in the melted butter. With a whisk, gently stir the flour into the eggs, gradually adding the rum (if using) and enough of the milk to make a smooth batter the consistency of single (light) cream. Stir in the desiccated coconut. If time allows, cover and leave to stand for about 15 minutes.
2. Lightly brush the crêpe maker or a non-stick frying pan with a little oil or melted butter. Preheat the crêpe maker to 'Medium', or put the non-stick frying pan over a medium heat.
3. When hot, pour a small ladleful of batter and spread or swirl to give a thin layer. Cook gently for about 30–45 seconds on one side until the underside is golden brown. Using a flat spatula or palette knife, carefully flip the galette over and cook the second side for about 30 seconds. Lift out and keep warm.
4. Cook the remaining batter and serve warm.

Breakfast Cinnamon Orange Waffles

What a good start to the day: hot sweet waffles and a strong espresso coffee.

Serves 4

115 g / 4 oz / 1 cup plain (all-purpose) flour
1 tsp baking powder
½ tsp ground cinnamon
Pinch of salt
3 tbsp muscovado sugar
2 medium eggs
2 tbsp melted butter
150 ml / ¼ pint / ⅔ cup unsweetened orange juice
150 ml / ¼ pint / ⅔ cup milk
Icing sugar, to dust

1. Sift the flour, baking powder, ground cinnamon and salt into a bowl and stir in the sugar. Make a well in the centre, break in the eggs and pour in the melted butter. With a whisk, gently stir the flour mixture into the eggs, gradually adding the orange juice and enough of the milk to make a smooth batter the consistency of double (heavy) cream.
2. Preheat the waffle maker to 'Medium' heat.
3. When at temperature, open the machine and pour a small ladleful of batter into the compartments, taking care not to overfill.
4. Close the machine and cook for 4–6 minutes until golden brown. Remove the waffles and immediately dust with icing sugar.
5. Cook the remaining batter, dust with icing sugar and serve warm.

Blinis with Grapes and Lemon Mascarpone

Blinis are traditional Russian yeasted pancakes usually served with smoked salmon. This quick, sweet, yeast-free version is perfect for afternoon tea.

Serves 4–6

Topping
200 g / 7 oz seedless green grapes
1 small lemon
175 g / 6 oz light mascarpone cheese
2 tbsp milk
1 tbsp clear honey

Blinis
115 g / 4 oz / 1 cup buckwheat flour
2 tsp baking powder
Pinch of salt
2 tbsp caster sugar
2 medium eggs
300 ml / ½ pint / 1¼ cups milk
Oil or melted butter

1. Slice or quarter the seedless grapes, cover and chill. Finely grate the rind from the lemon. Cut in half and squeeze out the juice.
2. Spoon the mascarpone cheese into a bowl and add the lemon juice, half the grated lemon rind (remainder for the waffle batter), milk and honey. Beat or whisk until light and fluffy. Cover and chill.

3. Sift the flour, baking powder and salt into a bowl and add the reserved grated lemon rind and sugar. Make a well in the centre and break in the eggs. With a whisk, gently stir the flour into the eggs, gradually adding enough of the milk to make a smooth batter the consistency of double (heavy) cream. If time allows, cover and leave to stand for about 15–30 minutes.

4. Lightly brush the crêpe maker or a non-stick frying pan with a little oil or melted butter. Preheat the crêpe maker to 'Medium', or put the non-stick frying pan over a medium heat.

5. When hot, pour in a small ladleful of batter and spread to make small 6 cm / 2½ inch blinis. Cook gently for about 30–45 seconds on one side until the underside is golden brown and small bubbles begin rising to the surface and burst. Using a flat spatula or palette knife, carefully flip the blini over and cook the second side for about 30 seconds. Lift out and keep warm.

6. Cook the remaining batter and keep warm. Spread the warm blinis with a little lemon mascarpone and top with pieces of grape.

Cherry Hotcakes

In place of the almond extract you could use 1 tbsp of chopped almonds or ground almonds.

Serves 4–6

250 g / 9 oz pitted cherries, thawed if frozen
115 g / 4 oz / 1 cup buckwheat flour
1 tsp baking powder
Pinch of salt
2 medium eggs
2 tbsp melted butter
A few drops almond extract
300 ml / ½ pint / 1¼ cups milk
Oil or melted butter
Icing sugar, to dust

1. If using thawed frozen cherries, drain if very wet. Roughly chop the cherries.
2. Sift the flour, baking powder and salt into a bowl. Make a well in the centre, break in the eggs, pour in the melted butter and add a few drops of almond extract. With a whisk, gently stir the flour into the eggs, gradually adding enough of the milk to make a smooth batter the consistency of double (heavy) cream. If time allows, cover and leave to stand for about 15 minutes.

3. Lightly brush the crêpe maker or a non-stick frying pan with a little oil or melted butter. Preheat the crêpe maker to 'Medium', or put the non-stick frying pan over a medium heat.

4. When hot, pour a small ladleful of batter and spread to give a small hotcake. Before the batter sets drop 2 or 3 pieces of cherries onto the surface and gently push into the batter. Cook gently for about 30–45 seconds on one side until the underside is golden brown. Using a flat spatula or palette knife, carefully flip the hotcake over and cook the second side for about 30–45 seconds. Lift out and keep warm.

5. Dust with icing sugar before serving.

Almond Waffles with Strawberries and Balsamic Syrup

A little Italian balsamic vinegar gives a subtle sweet/sour flavour that enhances the taste of strawberries.

Serves 4–6

Topping
350 g / 12 oz strawberries
4 tbsp caster sugar
3 tbsp balsamic vinegar

Waffles
55 g / 2 oz / ½ cup wholemeal (whole-wheat) flour
55 g / 2 oz / ½ cup buckwheat flour
1 tsp baking powder
Pinch of salt
3 tbsp caster sugar
2 medium eggs
2 tbsp melted butter
300 ml / ½ pint / 1¼ cups milk
50 g / 1¾ oz flaked (slivered) almonds
Icing sugar, to dust

1. Remove any stalks or leaves from the strawberries and cut into quarters. Put the sugar and balsamic vinegar into a bowl and stir to dissolve the sugar. Fold in the quartered strawberries. Cover and leave for the flavours to infuse. Stir once or twice to coat the strawberries in the syrup.

2. Sift the wholemeal (whole-wheat) flour, buckwheat flour, baking powder and salt into a bowl and stir in the sugar. Make a well in the centre, break in the eggs and pour in the melted butter. With a whisk, gently stir the flour mixture into the eggs, gradually adding enough of the milk to make a smooth batter the consistency of double (heavy) cream. Stir in the flaked (slivered) almonds.
3. Preheat the waffle maker to 'Medium' heat.
4. When at temperature, open the machine and pour a small ladleful of batter into the compartments, taking care not to overfill.
5. Close the machine and cook for 4–6 minutes until golden brown.
6. Cook the remaining batter, keep warm.
7. Dust the warm waffles with icing sugar and serve with the strawberries and balsamic syrup.

Spiced Apple Waffles

I think apple dishes flavoured with mixed spice have a warm wintry feel. Serve with syrup, crème fraîche or piping hot English custard.

Serves 4–6

Filling
1 eating apple

Waffles
55 g / 2 oz / ½ cup buckwheat flour
55 g / 2 oz / ½ cup cornmeal flour
1 tsp baking powder
Pinch of salt
3 tbsp golden caster sugar
2 medium eggs
2 tbsp melted butter
300 ml / ½ pint / 1¼ cups milk
Icing sugar, to dust

1. Peel, quarter, and core the apple. Cut into small pieces.
2. Sift the buckwheat flour, cornmeal, baking powder and salt into a bowl and stir in the sugar. Make a well in the centre, break in the eggs and pour in the melted butter. With a whisk, gently stir the flour mixture into the eggs, gradually adding enough of the milk to make a smooth batter the consistency of double (heavy) cream. Stir in the chopped apple.
3. Preheat the waffle maker to 'Medium' heat.
4. When at temperature, open the machine and pour a small ladleful of batter into the compartments, taking care not to overfill.
5. Close the machine and cook for 4–6 minutes until golden brown.
6. Cook the remaining batter and keep warm.
7. Dust the warm waffles with icing sugar and serve warm

4

Savoury Pancakes –
A Second Helping

ICTURE A PAINTER'S palette. It's great fun to surprise people with savoury waffles and pancakes in bright, vibrant colours. Just mix colourful ingredients into the fillings and toppings.

There's tomato juice for a rosy red colouring. For a touch of yellow, use a lemon. Spinach or herbs will produce various shades of green, and grated beetroot (beet) will give your crêpes a deep maroon hue. You don't have to be subtle or understated – good food can be a treat for the eye as well as for the appetite.

With several of these recipes, the topping can be prepared beforehand. If you do this, you can then complete the process for the topping while the waffles or pancakes are being made. For ease of reading, I haven't always included this alternative approach within the individual recipes.

Spiced Basil Waffles

Tomato juice with basil gives a Mediterranean flavour and a reddish colour to these waffles. The Worcestershire sauce adds spice.

Serves 4–6

Small bunch of basil leaves
115 g / 4 oz / 1 cup plain (all-purpose) flour
1 tsp baking powder
Pinch of salt
3 medium eggs
2 tbsp melted butter
150 ml / ¼ pint / ²/₃ cup tomato juice
½ tsp Worcestershire sauce
150 ml / ¼ pint / ²/₃ cup milk

1. Pull the basil leaves from the stalks and tear into small pieces.
2. Sift the flour, baking powder and salt into a bowl. Make a well in the centre, break in the eggs and pour in the melted butter. With a whisk, gently stir the flour mixture into the eggs, gradually adding the tomato juice, Worcestershire sauce and enough of the milk to make a smooth batter the consistency of double (heavy) cream. Stir in the torn basil.
3. Preheat the waffle maker to 'Medium' heat.
4. When at temperature, open the machine and pour a small ladleful of batter into the compartments, taking care not to overfill.
5. Close the machine and cook for 4–6 minutes until golden brown and crisp.
6. Cook the remaining batter, and serve warm.

Blinis, Smoked Salmon and Soured Cream

Blinis are Russian yeasted pancakes, topped with smoked salmon, soured cream and fish roe, and traditionally made with buckwheat flour. Mine use a yeasted batter, but you can use baking powder as the raising agent. As blinis are small, several can be cooked at the same time. Freeze the remainder in small batches.

Topping to serve 6–8 as appetizers

Blinis
55 g / 2 oz / ½ cup buckwheat flour
55 g / 2 oz / ½ cup plain (all-purpose) flour
¼ tsp salt
½ tsp caster sugar
½ tsp fast-action dried yeast
2 medium eggs
2 tbsp melted butter
2 tbsp finely chopped dill
300 ml / ½ pint / 1¼ cups milk
Oil or melted butter

Topping
200 g / 7 oz smoked salmon
Sprigs of dill
300 ml / ½ pint / generous 1¼ cups soured cream
Small amount of salmon roe, optional
Freshly milled black pepper
Lemon wedges, to squeeze over

1. Sift the buckwheat flour, plain (all-purpose) flour and salt into a bowl and add the sugar. Stir in the yeast. Make a well in the centre and break in the eggs, pour in the melted butter and add the chopped dill. With a whisk, gently stir the flour into the eggs, gradually adding enough of the milk to make a smooth batter the consistency of single (light) cream. Cover the bowl with oiled clear film (plastic wrap) and leave in a warm place until doubled in size, about 45 minutes to an hour. Before using, mix the batter and, if too thick, stir in a little milk.
2. Lightly brush the crêpe maker or a non-stick frying pan with a little oil or melted butter. Preheat the crêpe maker to 'Medium', or put the non-stick frying pan over a medium heat.
3. When hot, pour in a spoonful of batter and spread out to about 4–6 cm / 2–2½ inches across. As the blinis are small, cook several at the same time. Cook gently for about 30–45 seconds on one side until the underside is golden brown. Using a flat spatula or palette knife, carefully flip the blinis over and cook the second side for about 30 seconds. Lift out and keep warm.
4. Cook the remaining batter and keep warm.
5. Prepare the topping just before the blinis are cooked. Cut the salmon into strips and pull the dill leaves from the stalks.
6. Put salmon strips and a spoonful of soured cream on top of each blini. Add a little salmon roe, if using. Season with a little pepper and add a dill leaf. Serve with lemon wedges, to squeeze over.

Chestnut Flour Waffles with Mushrooms

These waffles make me think of autumn, with their flour made from chestnuts and earthy mushrooms in the Italian way. Use your favourite selection of mushrooms.

Serves 4

Waffles
55 g / 2 oz / ½ cup chestnut flour
55 g / 2 oz / ½ cup plain (all-purpose) flour
1 tsp baking powder
Pinch of salt
2 medium eggs
1 tbsp melted butter
300 ml / ½ pint / 1¼ cups milk

Topping
2 shallots
350 g / 12 oz mixed mushrooms, such as button, oyster, chestnut,
   shiitake
1 tbsp olive oil
4 tbsp vegetable stock
2 tsp lemon juice
Freshly milled salt and black pepper
1 tbsp chopped parsley

1. Sift the chestnut flour, plain (all-purpose) flour, baking powder and salt into a bowl. Make a well in the centre, break in the eggs and pour in the melted butter. With a whisk, gently stir the flour mixture into the eggs, gradually adding enough of the milk to make a

smooth batter the consistency of double (heavy) cream.

2. Preheat the waffle maker to 'Medium' heat.

3. When at temperature, open the machine and pour a small ladleful of batter into the compartments, taking care not to overfill.

4. Close the machine and cook for 4–6 minutes until golden brown.

5. Cook the remaining batter and serve warm.

6. To make the topping. Finely chop the shallots. Trim the mushrooms and cut in half, or slice if large.

7. Heat the oil in a frying pan and cook the chopped shallots for 5 minutes until softened without browning. Add the mushrooms and fry until golden. Stir in the vegetable stock, lemon juice, a little seasoning and parsley. Cook for 1–2 minutes until piping hot and serve with the warm waffles.

Spinach Pancakes with Tomatoes

Red tomatoes are a striking contrast to the deep green spinach. You can always add a little fish or meat to the filling.

Serves 4

Filling
14 oz / 400 g cherry tomatoes
1 tsp olive oil
2 tbsp red pesto
Freshly milled pepper

Pancakes
50 g / 1¾ oz fresh spinach leaves, or frozen
150 ml / ¼ pint / ²/₃ cup milk
115 g / 4 oz / 1 cup plain (all-purpose) flour
Pinch of salt
2 medium eggs
Oil or melted butter

1. Cut the tomatoes in half. Heat the oil and pesto in a pan, add the tomato halves and cook for a few minutes until cooked. Season with a little black pepper.
2. Cook the fresh spinach leaves in 1 tbsp water until wilted. Whiz with a stick-blender until a purée. Pour into a jug and make up to 300 ml / ½ pint / 1¼ cups with the milk added to the spinach.

3. Sift the flour and salt into a bowl. Make a well in the centre and break in the eggs. With a whisk, gently stir the flour into the eggs, gradually adding the spinach and milk mixture to make a smooth batter the consistency of single (light) cream. Add a little more milk, if necessary. If time allows, cover and leave to stand for about 30 minutes.

4. Lightly brush the crêpe maker or a non-stick frying pan with a little oil or melted butter. Preheat the crêpe maker to 'Medium', or put the non-stick frying pan over a medium heat.

5. When hot, pour a small ladleful of batter and spread or swirl to give a thin layer. Cook gently for about 30–45 seconds on one side until the underside is golden brown. Using a flat spatula or palette knife, carefully flip the pancake over and cook the second side for about 30 seconds. Lift out and keep warm.

6. Cook the remaining batter and keep warm.

7. To serve, spoon the tomato filling onto the warm pancakes. Fold the pancake over the filling and serve immediately.

Five-Spice Duck Pancakes

The spicing gives a Far–Eastern feel to these pancakes. Serve with a little plum sauce.

Serve 4–6

Filling
3 skinless duck breasts
3 tsp five-spice powder
1 tbsp cornflour (cornstarch)
3 spring onions (scallions)
2 courgettes (zucchini)
2 tbsp oil
Large handful of bean sprouts
150 ml / ¼ pint / ⅔ cup vegetable stock
1 tsp soy sauce

Pancakes
55 g / 2 oz / ½ cup rice flour
55 g / 2 oz / ½ cup plain (all-purpose) flour
Pinch of salt
2 medium eggs
300 ml / ½ pint / 1¼ cups milk
Oil or melted butter

1. Cut the duck breast into very thin strips and put them into a bowl. Add the five-spice powder and cornflour (cornstarch) and stir to coat the meat in the spices. Cover and chill until needed. Cut the spring onions (scallions) and courgettes (zucchini) into thin strips.
2. Sift the rice flour and plain (all-purpose) flour into a bowl and add the salt. Make a well in the centre and break in the eggs. With a whisk, gently stir the flour into the eggs, gradually adding enough of the milk to make a smooth batter the consistency of single (light) cream. If time allows, cover and leave to stand for about 15 minutes.

3. Lightly brush the crêpe maker or a non-stick frying pan with a little oil or melted butter. Preheat the crêpe maker to 'Medium', or put the non-stick frying pan over a medium heat.

4. When hot, pour a small ladleful of batter and spread or swirl to give a thin layer. Cook gently for about 30–45 seconds on one side until the underside is golden brown. Using a flat spatula or palette knife, carefully flip the pancake over and cook the second side for about 30 seconds. Lift out and keep warm.

5. Cook the remaining batter and serve warm.

6. For the filling: heat the oil in a large pan and stir-fry the duck strips a few at a time until golden and cooked through. Lift out of the pan and stir-fry the strips of spring onions (scallions) and courgettes (zucchini) for 3–4 minutes.

7. Stir in the cooked strips of duck, bean sprouts, vegetable stock and soy sauce. Stirring, cook over a high heat for 3–4 minutes until piping hot and cooked through.

8. Spoon the sauce and vegetables onto the warm pancakes and roll or fold over.

Pea, Soured Cream and Corn Waffles

Turmeric adds yellow colouring to these waffles.

Serves 4–6

115 g / 4 oz / 1 cup plain (all-purpose) flour
1 tsp baking powder
¼ tsp turmeric
Pinch of salt
2 medium eggs
2 tbsp melted butter
3 tbsp soured cream
300 ml / ½ pint / 1¼ cups milk, less 3 tbsp
100 g / 3½ oz peas
100 g / 3½ oz sweetcorn

1. Sift the flour, baking powder, turmeric and salt into a bowl. Make a well in the centre, break in the eggs and pour in the melted butter. With a whisk, gently stir the flour mixture into the eggs, gradually adding the soured cream and enough of the milk to make a smooth batter the consistency of single (light) cream. Stir in the peas and sweetcorn.
2. Preheat the waffle maker to 'Medium' heat.
3. When at temperature, open the machine and pour a small ladleful of batter into the compartments, taking care not to overfill.
4. Close the machine and cook for 4–6 minutes until golden brown.
5. Cook the remaining batter, and serve warm.

Watercress, Red (Bell) Pepper and Cornmeal Waffles

Pungent, peppery and brightly-coloured waffles.

Serves 4–6

½ red (bell) pepper
1 small bunch of watercress
115 g / 4 oz / 1 cup cornmeal flour
1 tsp baking powder
Pinch of salt
2 medium eggs
2 tbsp melted butter
300 ml / ½ pint / 1¼ cups milk

1. Remove and discard the seeds from the red (bell) pepper and cut into small dice. Put into a microwave-proof dish, pour over 1 tbsp water, cover and cook in a microwave oven on a low power for a few seconds. Drain, rinse in cold water, drain and leave until cold. Pull the leaves from the watercress and chop.
2. Sift the flour, baking powder and salt into a bowl. Make a well in the centre, break in the eggs and pour in the melted butter. With a whisk, gently stir the flour mixture into the eggs, gradually adding enough of the milk to make a smooth batter the consistency of double (heavy) cream. Stir in the chopped watercress and diced red (bell) pepper.
3. Preheat the waffle maker to 'Medium' heat.
4. When at temperature, open the machine and pour a small ladleful of batter into the compartments, taking care not to overfill.
5. Close the machine and cook for 4–6 minutes until golden brown.
6. Cook the remaining batter, and serve warm.

Beer Batter Pancakes with Steak

Beer in a pancake, wrapped around a steak – what a combination!

Serves 4

Pancakes
115 g / 4 oz / 1 cup plain (all-purpose) flour
Pinch of salt
2 medium eggs
1 tbsp melted butter
150 ml / ¼ pint / ²/₃ cup beer
150 ml / ¼ pint / ²/₃ cup milk

Filling
4 beef-steaks
Oil
Freshly milled salt and black pepper
4 slices blue cheese
Rocket (arugula) leaves

1. Sift the flour into a bowl and add the salt. Make a well in the centre, break in the eggs and pour in the melted butter. With a whisk, gently stir the flour into the eggs, gradually adding the beer and enough of the milk to make a smooth batter the consistency of single (light) cream. If time allows, cover and leave to stand for about 15 minutes.
2. Lightly brush the crêpe maker or a non-stick frying pan with a little oil or melted butter. Preheat the crêpe maker to 'Medium', or put the non-stick frying pan over a medium heat.

3. When hot, pour a ladleful of batter and spread or swirl to make a large pancake. Cook gently for about 30–45 seconds on one side until the underside is golden brown. Using a flat spatula or palette knife, carefully flip the pancake over and cook the second side for about 30 seconds. Lift out and keep warm.
4. Cook the remaining batter. You will need 4 large warmed pancakes.
5. Brush the steaks with a little oil and season with a little salt and pepper. Put under a hot grill (broiler) and cook to your liking. Top each steak with a slice of blue cheese and cook for a few seconds for the cheese to begin to melt.
6. Lift the steaks onto the warm pancakes and add some of the rocket (arugula) leaves. Fold the pancake over the steak and serve immediately.

Lemon Crêpes with Smoked Trout, Crème Fraîche and Fennel Leaves

Serve with salad and lemon wedges. Horseradish is surprisingly good with oily fish.

Serves 4

Filling
Small bunch of fennel leaves
3 hot-smoked trout fillets
150 ml / ¼ pint crème fraîche
2 tbsp capers, optional
2 tsp horseradish sauce
Freshly milled black pepper

Crêpes
115 g / 4 oz / 1 cup plain buckwheat flour
Pinch of salt
2 tsp grated lemon rind
2 medium eggs
1 tbsp melted butter
300 ml / ½ pint / 1¼ cups milk
Oil or melted butter

1. Pull the fennel leaves from the stalks and roughly chop. Remove any skin and bones from the trout fillets and flake the fish.
2. Spoon the crème fraîche and capers, if using, into a bowl. Stir in the horseradish sauce and a little black pepper. Gently fold in the flaked trout. Cover and chill until needed.

3. Sift the flour and salt into a bowl and add the lemon rind. Make a well in the centre, break in the eggs and pour in the melted butter. With a whisk, gently stir the buckwheat flour into the eggs, gradually adding enough of the milk to make a smooth batter the consistency of single (light) cream. If time allows, cover and leave to stand for about 15 minutes.
4. Lightly brush the crêpe maker or a non-stick frying pan with a little oil or melted butter. Preheat the crêpe maker to 'Medium', or put the non-stick frying pan over a medium heat.
5. When hot, pour a small ladleful of batter and spread or swirl to give a thin layer. Cook gently for about 30–45 seconds on one side until the underside is golden brown. Using a flat spatula or palette knife, carefully flip the crêpe over and cook the second side for about 30 seconds. Lift out and keep warm.
6. Cook the remaining batter and keep warm.
7. Spoon the trout mixture onto the warm crêpes and roll or fold over.

Green Crêpes with Guacamole

Guacamole is a Mexican favourite, made with crushed avocado.

Serves 4–6

Filling
2 large ripe avocados
2 tbsp lime juice
1 green chilli (see page 8)
Small bunch of coriander (cilantro)
1 small onion
1 garlic clove
2–3 tbsp olive oil
Freshly milled black pepper

Crêpes
115 g / 4 oz / 1 cup plain (all-purpose) flour
Pinch of salt
4 tbsp freeze-dried chopped chervil or parsley
2 medium eggs
2 tbsp melted butter
300 ml / ½ pint / 1¼ cups milk
Oil or melted butter

1. Cut each avocado in half lengthways and twist the two halves to separate. Remove the stones (pits). Peel the avocados and put the flesh into a bowl. Immediately pour over the lime juice and, with a fork or potato masher, crush the avocados.
2. Cut the chilli in half, remove and discard the stalk and seeds. Pull the leaves from the coriander (cilantro) stalks.
3. Finely chop the chilli, onion, garlic and coriander (cilantro) leaves, by hand or in a food processor, and stir into the crushed avocado. Stir in olive oil and season to taste. Cover tightly and chill.

4. Sift the flour into a bowl and add the salt and the chopped chervil or parsley. Make a well in the centre, break in the eggs and pour in the butter. With a whisk, gently stir the flour into the eggs, gradually adding enough of the milk to make a smooth batter the consistency of single (light) cream. If time allows, cover and leave to stand for about 15 minutes.
5. Lightly brush the crêpe maker or a large non-stick frying pan with a little oil or melted butter. Preheat the crêpe maker to 'Medium', or put the non-stick frying pan over a medium heat.
6. When hot, pour a small ladleful of batter and spread or swirl to give a thin layer. Cook gently for about 30–45 seconds on one side until the underside is golden brown. Using a flat spatula or palette knife, carefully flip the crêpe over and cook the second side for about 30 seconds. Lift out and keep warm.
7. Cook the remaining batter and keep warm.
8. Spread some of the guacamole over each pancake to the edges and fold into quarters.

Potato and Ham Waffles

Choose floury potatoes for best results. Serve as part of breakfast or brunch, or as an accompaniment to grilled meat or fish.

Serves 4–6

2 rashers (strips) smoked back bacon
140 g / 5 oz cooked potato
55 g / 4 oz / ½ cup plain (all-purpose) flour
1 tsp baking powder
Pinch of salt
2 medium eggs
2 tbsp melted butter
300 ml / ½ pint / 1¼ cups milk
Oil or melted butter

1. Trim any fat from the bacon rashers (strips) and grill (broil) until cooked. Drain on kitchen paper (paper towels) and finely chop.
2. Put the potato into a bowl and finely mash (you don't want lumps).
3. Sift the flour, baking powder and salt over the mashed potato. Make a well in the centre, break in the eggs and pour in the melted butter. With a spoon, stir the potato mixture into the eggs, gradually adding enough of the milk to make a smooth batter the consistency of double (heavy) cream. Stir in the chopped bacon.
4. Preheat the waffle maker to 'Medium' heat.
5. When at temperature, open the machine and pour a small ladleful of batter into the compartments, taking care not to overfill.
6. Close the machine and cook for 4–6 minutes until golden brown.
7. Cook the remaining batter and serve warm.

Prawn (Shrimp), Parmesan and Chive Waffles

These waffles are not suitable for freezing. In place of the prawns (shrimps), you could use small pieces of white fish or other shellfish. Serve with lemon.

Serves 4–6

140 g / 5 oz shelled prawns (shrimps)
Small bunch of chives
115 g / 4 oz / 1 cup plain (all-purpose) flour
1 tsp baking powder
Pinch of salt
2 medium eggs
2 tbsp melted butter
300 ml / ½ pint / 1¼ cups milk
1 tbsp Parmesan cheese

1. Roughly chop the prawns (shrimps) and drain on kitchen paper (paper towels) if wet. Finely chop the chives.
2. Sift the flour, baking powder and salt into a bowl. Make a well in the centre, break in the eggs and pour in the melted butter. With a whisk, gently stir the flour mixture into the eggs, gradually adding enough of the milk to make a smooth batter the consistency of double (heavy) cream. Stir in the prawns (shrimps), chives and Parmesan cheese.
3. Preheat the waffle maker to 'Medium' heat.
4. When at temperature, open the machine and pour a small ladleful of batter into the compartments, taking care not to overfill.
5. Close the machine and cook for 4–6 minutes until golden brown.
6. Cook the remaining batter and serve warm.

Beetroot (Beet) Crêpes with Roasted Vegetables

Deep maroon in colour, with a spicy and earthy appeal. Great for vegetarians.

Serves 4

Filling

400 g / 14 oz bag of mixed roasted vegetables, frozen
2 tsp oil
1 tbsp grated fresh ginger
3 tbsp wholegrain mustard
1 tsp liquid vegetable stock
Freshly milled salt and black pepper

Crêpes

½ small cooked beetroot (beet), about 50 g / 1¾ oz
115 g / 4 oz / 1 cup plain (all-purpose) flour
Pinch of salt
2 medium eggs
1 tbsp melted butter
300 ml / ½ pint / 1¼ cups milk
Oil or melted butter
Soured cream, to serve

1. The vegetables can be cooked from frozen – cut any large pieces in half. Heat the oil in a pan and stir in the roasted vegetables, grated ginger, mustard and vegetable stock. Cook over a medium-high heat until the vegetables are piping hot and most of the liquid has evaporated. Season with salt and pepper, if necessary.
2. Finely grate the beetroot (beet). It's a good idea to wear disposable gloves as it will stain your fingers.

3. Sieve the flour and salt into a bowl. Make a well in the centre, break in the eggs and pour in the melted butter. With a whisk, gently stir the flour into the eggs, gradually adding enough of the milk to make a smooth batter the consistency of single (light) cream. Stir in the grated beetroot (beet). If time allows, cover and leave to stand for about 15–30 minutes.

4. Lightly brush the crêpe maker or a non-stick frying pan with a little oil or melted butter. Preheat the crêpe maker to 'Medium', or put the non-stick frying pan over a medium heat.

5. When hot, pour a small ladleful of batter and spread or swirl to give a thin layer. Cook gently for about 30–45 seconds on one side until the underside is golden brown. Using a flat spatula or palette knife, carefully flip the crêpe over and cook the second side for about 20 seconds.

6. Spoon some of the roasted vegetable mixture in the centre of a crêpe. Add a blob of soured cream and fold the crêpe in over the filling. Serve immediately.

Toasted Pancake 'Sandwich'

A cheesy chicken sandwich with no bread. Just a bit of fun.

Serves 4

Filling
2 tomatoes
5 slices cooked roast chicken
225 g / 8 oz Manchego cheese, or other hard cheese such as
    Red Leicester or Cheddar
4 tbsp cucumber relish

Pancakes
115 g / 4 oz / 1 cup wholemeal (whole-wheat) flour
Pinch of salt
2 medium eggs
300 ml / ½ pint / 1¼ cups milk
Oil or melted butter

1. Finely chop the tomatoes and the roast chicken. Grate the cheese into a bowl and add the chopped tomato, chicken and cucumber relish. Mix thoroughly, cover and chill.
2. Sift the flour and salt into a bowl. Make a well in the centre and break in the eggs. With a whisk, gently stir the flour into the eggs, gradually adding enough of the milk to make a smooth batter the consistency of single (light) cream. If time allows, cover and leave to stand for about 15 minutes.
3. Lightly brush the crêpe maker or a non-stick frying pan with a little oil or melted butter. Preheat the crêpe maker to 'Medium', or put the non-stick frying pan over a medium heat.

4. When hot, pour a small ladleful of batter and spread or swirl to give a layer, not too thin, 15 cm / 6 inches across. Cook gently for about 30–45 seconds on one side until the underside is golden brown. Using a flat spatula or palette knife, carefully flip the pancake over and cook the second side for only a few seconds until set, but not browned. Lift out and cook the remaining batter, making about 8–10 pancakes in total.

5. Put a pancake pale-side down on a board and spread the browned side with a little chicken filling. Cover with a second pancake browned side down. Repeat with the remaining pancakes and filling.

6. Brush the hot crêpe maker or frying pan with a little more melted butter, and when hot put the pancake 'sandwich' onto the hot surface. Cook for 30–40 seconds until browned, then carefully turn over and cook until the last side is brown and the filling is piping hot. Reduce the temperature if the pancake browns too much.

Courgette (Zucchini) Hotcakes

These hotcakes have strips of courgette (zucchini) sunk into the batter. If using regular-sized courgettes, cut into round slices rather than lengthways. Or you could use sliced mushrooms or (bell) peppers instead.

Serves 4–6

6–8 mini courgettes (zucchini)
115 g / 4 oz / 1 cup buckwheat flour
¼ tsp baking powder
Pinch of salt
3 medium eggs
1 tbsp melted butter
300 ml / ½ pint / 1¼ cups milk
Oil or melted butter

1. Slice the courgettes (zucchini) lengthways. Blanch in boiling water (from the kettle) for 45 seconds, or until just tender. Drain and spread out on kitchen paper (paper towels) to absorb excess liquid.
2. Sift the flour, baking powder and salt into a bowl. Make a well in the centre, break in the eggs and pour in the melted butter. With a whisk, gently stir the flour into the eggs, gradually adding enough of the milk to make a smooth batter the consistency of double (heavy) cream. If time allows, cover and leave to stand for about 15 minutes.
3. Lightly brush the crêpe maker or a non-stick frying pan with a little oil or melted butter. Preheat the crêpe maker to 'Medium', or put the non-stick frying pan over a medium heat.
4. When hot, pour a small ladleful of batter and spread to give a hotcake about 10 cm / 4 inches across. Before the batter has set, put some courgette (zucchini) slices onto the crêpe and gently push into the batter. Cook gently for about 30–45 seconds on one side until the underside is golden brown. Using a flat spatula or palette knife, carefully flip the crêpe over and cook the second side for about 30 seconds. Lift out and keep warm.
5. Cook the remaining batter and serve warm.

5
Sweet Pancakes – A Second Helping

THERE ARE SO MANY delicious and mouthwatering flavours to choose from here. These pancakes and waffles abound in honey, syrup and nuts, fruit and spices. They are perfect for special occasions and will brighten up an ordinary day.

Among others, look out for crêpe suzette (an established favourite), tiramisu pancakes (coffee-flavoured and rather indulgent), munchable waffles made with oatmeal, apple and cinnamon, and a showpiece chocolate pancake stack.

These are luxurious treats, with more than a hint of sophistication, yet so easy to make using your waffle maker and crêpe maker, or a non-stick frying pan. Who can resist a second helping?

Oatmeal, Apple and Cinnamon Waffles

Oatmeal gives an interesting texture to these waffles. You can use a firm pear in place of the apple. Serve with crème fraîche or a caramel sauce.

Serves 4–6

1 small eating apple
55 g / 2 oz / ½ cup plain (all-purpose) flour
1 tsp baking powder
½ tsp ground cinnamon
Pinch of salt
55 g / 2 oz / ½ cup fine-medium oatmeal
3 tbsp light brown sugar
2 medium eggs
2 tbsp melted butter
300 ml / ½ pint / 1¼ cups milk

1. Peel, core and finely chop the apple.
2. Sift the flour, baking powder, ground cinnamon and salt into a bowl and stir in the oatmeal and sugar. Make a well in the centre, break in the eggs and pour in the melted butter. With a whisk, gently stir the flour mixture into the eggs, gradually adding enough of the milk to make a smooth batter the consistency of single (light) cream. Stir in the chopped apple.
3. Preheat the waffle maker to 'Medium' heat.
4. When at temperature, open the machine and pour a small ladleful of batter into the compartments, taking care not to overfill.
5. Close the machine and cook for 4–6 minutes until golden brown.
6. Cook the remaining batter, and serve warm.

Crêpes Suzette

A classic dish, finished off at the table in top-class restaurants. The crêpes are warmed in an orange sauce and then flambéed in Grand Marnier.

Filling serves 4 – uses 8 of the crêpes about 10 cm / 4 inches across

1 large orange

Crêpes
115 g / 4 oz / 1 cup plain (all-purpose) flour
Pinch of salt
1 tbsp caster sugar
1 medium egg
300 ml / ½ pint / 1¼ cups milk
Oil or melted butter

Filling
140 g / 5 oz unsalted butter
3 tbsp caster sugar
3 tbsp Grand Marnier or orange liqueur

1. Finely grate the rind from the orange, cut in half and squeeze out the juice. Reserve the juices and all but 2 tsp of the grated orange rind.
2. Sift the flour into a bowl and add the salt, sugar and 2 tsp of the orange rind. Make a well in the centre and break in the egg. With a whisk, gently stir the flour into the egg, gradually adding enough of the milk to make a smooth batter the consistency of single (light) cream. If time allows, cover and leave to stand for about 30 minutes.

3. Lightly brush the crêpe maker or a non-stick frying pan with a little oil or melted butter. Preheat the crêpe maker to 'Medium', or put the non-stick frying pan over a medium heat.

4. When hot, pour a small ladleful of batter and spread or swirl to give a thin layer. Cook gently for about 30–45 seconds on one side until the underside is golden brown. Using a flat spatula or palette knife, carefully flip the crêpe over and cook the second side for about 30 seconds and lift out of the pan.

5. Cook the remaining batter, making 8 crêpes in total. Fold each crêpe in half and then half again.

6. Melt the butter into a very large frying pan. Add the sugar and stir until melted. Stir in the reserved orange rind and juice, heat until bubbling and thickened.

7. Put a folded crêpe into the pan and quickly turn it over in the hot sauce. Repeat with the remaining crêpes. Keep spooning the sauce over the crêpes as they heat through.

8. Pour the Grand Marnier over the crêpes and carefully set alight. As soon as the flames have died down, serve the crêpes with the sauce spooned over.

Pancakes with Fruits soaked in Earl Grey Tea

Using tea bags is an easy way to add flavour to this fruity pancake. Serve with scoops of vanilla ice cream or natural yogurt.

Serves 4–6

Filling
2 Earl Grey tea bags
4 dried, ready-to-eat apricots
250 g / 9 oz dried mixed fruit
½ tsp ground mixed spice
140 g / 5 oz chopped walnuts
1 tbsp brandy or orange juice

Pancakes
55 g / 2 oz / ½ cup wholemeal (whole-wheat) flour
55 g / 2 oz / ½ cup plain (all-purpose) flour
¼ tsp ground mixed spice
Pinch of salt
1 tbsp light brown sugar
2 medium eggs
300 ml / ½ pint / 1¼ cups milk
Oil or melted butter
Icing sugar, to dust

1. Drop the tea bags into a large bowl and pour over 150 ml / ¼ pint / ²/₃ cup boiling water (from the kettle). Leave for 15 minutes until quite strong. Remove and squeeze out the teabags.

2. Finely chop the dried, ready-to-eat apricots and put into the bowl of tea. Stir in the dried mixed fruit, ground mixed spice, chopped walnuts, and the brandy or orange juice. Mix all the ingredients together, cover and leave to stand for several hours or overnight, if possible. The fruits will absorb the liquid.

3. Sift the wholemeal (whole-wheat) flour, plain (all-purpose) flour, ground mixed spice and salt into a bowl. Stir in the sugar. Make a well in the centre and break in the eggs. With a whisk, gently stir the flour into the eggs, gradually adding enough of the milk to make a smooth batter the consistency of single (light) cream. If time allows, cover and leave to stand for about 15–30 minutes.

4. Lightly brush the crêpe maker or a non-stick frying pan with a little oil or melted butter. Preheat the crêpe maker to 'Medium', or put the non-stick frying pan over a medium heat.

5. When hot, pour a small ladleful of batter and spread or swirl to give a thin layer. Cook gently for about 30–45 seconds on one side until the underside is golden brown. Using a flat spatula or palette knife, carefully flip the pancake over and cook the second side for about 30 seconds. Lift out and keep warm.

6. Cook the remaining batter, and serve warm.

7. Spread some of the fruit filling over the warm pancakes and fold or roll. Dust with icing sugar.

Pineapple, Ginger and Coconut Waffles

A wonderful combination of flavours. Serve with golden syrup or pancake syrup with a little rum stirred in.

Serves 4–6

2 pineapple rings
Small piece of crystallized ginger, about 20 g / ¾ oz
115 g / 4 oz / 1 cup plain (all-purpose) flour
1 tsp baking powder
Pinch of salt
3 tbsp caster sugar
2 medium eggs
2 tbsp melted butter
300 ml / ½ pint / 1¼ cups milk
3 tbsp desiccated coconut

1. Finely chop the pineapple rings and the crystallized ginger.
2. Sift the flour, baking powder and salt into a bowl and stir in the sugar. Make a well in the centre, break in the eggs and pour in the melted butter. With a whisk, gently stir the flour mixture into the eggs, gradually adding enough of the milk to make a smooth batter the consistency of double (heavy) cream. Stir in the chopped pineapple rings, crystallized ginger and desiccated coconut.

3. Preheat the waffle maker to 'Medium' heat.
4. When at temperature, open the machine and pour a small ladleful of batter into the compartments, taking care not to overfill.
5. Close the machine and cook for 4–6 minutes until golden brown.
6. Cook the remaining batter, making about 8–10 waffles in total, and serve warm.

White Chocolate, Raspberry and Pistachio Waffles

A touch of luxury. Serve with ice cream or pouring cream.

Makes about 8–10 waffles

Small handful of raspberries
115 g / 4 oz / 1 cup plain (all-purpose) flour
1 tsp baking powder
Pinch of salt
3 tbsp caster sugar
2 medium eggs
2 tbsp melted butter
300 ml / ½ pint / 1¼ cups milk
60 g / 2¼ oz white chocolate chips
2 tbsp chopped pistachio nuts

1. Roughly chop the raspberries.
2. Sift the flour, baking powder and salt into a bowl and stir in the sugar. Make a well in the centre, break in the eggs and pour in the melted butter. With a whisk, gently stir the flour mixture into the eggs, gradually adding enough of the milk to make a smooth batter the consistency of double (heavy) cream. Stir in the raspberries, chocolate chips and pistachio nuts.

3. Preheat the waffle maker to 'Medium' heat.
4. When at temperature, open the machine and pour a small ladleful of batter into the compartments, taking care not to overfill.
5. Close the machine and cook for 4–6 minutes until golden brown.
6. Cook the remaining batter, making about 8–10 waffles in total, and serve warm.

Lemon and Lime Saucy Crêpes

My non-alcoholic version of crêpes suzette – no flambéing required.

Filling serves 4 – uses 8 of the crêpes about 10 cm / 4 inches across

1 large lemon
1 lime

Crêpes
115 g / 4 oz / 1 cup plain (all-purpose) flour
Pinch of salt
1 tbsp light brown sugar
1 medium egg
300 ml / ½ pint / 1¼ cups milk
Oil or melted butter

Filling
140 g / 5 oz unsalted butter
3 tbsp caster sugar
Small handful toasted flaked (slivered) almonds

1. Finely grate the rind from the lemon and the lime, cut both in half and squeeze out the juices. Reserve all but 1 tsp of the grated lemon rind and 1 tsp of the lime rind, and the juices.
2. Sift the flour into a bowl and add the salt, sugar and 1 tsp of the lemon rind and 1 tsp of the lime rind. Make a well in the centre and break in the egg. With a whisk, gently stir the flour into the egg, gradually adding enough of the milk to make a smooth batter the consistency of single (light) cream. If time allows, cover and leave to stand for about 30 minutes.
3. Lightly brush the crêpe maker or a non-stick frying pan with a little oil or melted butter. Preheat the crêpe maker to 'Medium', or put the non-stick frying pan over a medium heat.

4. When hot, pour a small ladleful of batter and spread or swirl to give a thin layer. Cook gently for about 30–45 seconds on one side until the underside is golden brown. Using a flat spatula or palette knife, carefully flip the crêpe over and cook the second side for about 30 seconds and lift out of the pan.
5. Cook the remaining batter, making 8 crêpes in total. Fold each crêpe in half and then half again.
6. Melt the butter into a very large frying pan. Add the sugar and stir until melted. Stir in the reserved lemon rind, lime rind and the lemon and lime juices. Heat until bubbling and thickened. Stir in the flaked (slivered) almonds
7. Put a folded crêpe into the pan and quickly turn it over in the hot sauce. Repeat with the remaining crêpes. Keep spooning the sauce over the crêpes as they heat through.
8. Serve the crêpes with the sauce spooned over.

Crêpe Parcels with Mozzarella Cheese and Cranberries

The mozzarella melts inside these scrumptious little parcels.

Serves 4

Filling
280 g / 10 oz cranberries
3 tbsp light brown sugar
200 g / 7 oz mozzarella cheese

Crêpes
115 g / 4 oz / 1 cup plain (all-purpose) flour
Pinch of salt
1 tbsp caster sugar
1 medium egg
300 ml / ½ pint / 1¼ cups milk
Oil or melted butter
Icing sugar, to dust

1. Tip the cranberries and sugar into a small pan. Pour over 2–3 tbsp water and gently cook until the cranberries are soft and the mixture isn't too wet. Leave until cold. Tear the mozzarella cheese into small pieces. Stir the pieces into the cold cranberries, cover and chill.
2. Sift the flour and salt into a bowl and stir in the sugar. Make a well in the centre and break in the egg. With a whisk, gently stir the flour into the egg, gradually adding enough of the milk to make a smooth batter the consistency of single (light) cream. If time allows, cover and leave to stand for about 30 minutes.
3. Lightly brush the crêpe maker or a non-stick frying pan with a little oil or melted butter. Preheat the crêpe maker to 'Medium', or put the non-stick frying pan over a medium heat.

4. When hot, pour a small ladleful of batter and spread or swirl to give a thin layer, about 18 cm / 7 inches across. Cook gently for about 30–45 seconds on one side until the underside is golden brown. Using a flat spatula or palette knife, carefully flip the crêpe over and cook the second side for only a second until set, but not browned. Lift out and cook the remaining batter.

5. Put the crêpes pale-side down on a board.

6. Put a spoonful of the cranberry mixture in the centre of each crêpe. Fold two opposite sides into the centre and fold the other two sides over to make a parcel. Turn them over, seam-side down, and gently press to neaten the shape.

7. Brush the hot crêpe maker or frying pan with a little more melted butter, and when hot put the crêpe 'parcels' onto the hot surface. Cook for 30–40 seconds until browned, then carefully turn over and cook until the last side is brown and the filling is hot and melting. Reduce the temperature if the crêpes brown too much.

Lemony Almond Waffles

Ground almonds with lemon – simple, but really stylish.

Serves 4–6

1 small lemon
55 g / 2 oz / ½ cup plain (all-purpose) flour
1 tbsp buckwheat flour
1 tsp baking powder
Pinch of salt
55 g / 2 oz ground almonds
3 tbsp caster sugar
2 medium eggs
2 tbsp melted butter
300 ml / ½ pint / 1¼ cups milk

1. Grate the rind from the lemon, cut in half and squeeze out the juice.
2. Sift the flours, baking powder and salt into a bowl and stir in the ground almonds and sugar. Make a well in the centre, break in the eggs, pour in the melted butter and add the grated lemon rind and juice. With a whisk, gently stir the flour mixture into the eggs, gradually adding enough of the milk to make a smooth batter the consistency of double (heavy) cream.
3. Preheat the waffle maker to 'Medium' heat.
4. When at temperature, open the machine and pour a small ladleful of batter into the compartments, taking care not to overfill.
5. Close the machine and cook for 4–6 minutes until golden brown.
6. Cook the remaining batter, and serve warm.

Elderflower Waffles with Pecan Nuts

Buttery rich pecan nuts and perfumed elderflower syrup – an unusual combination which works really well.

Serves 4–6

70 g / 2½ oz pecan nuts
115 g / 4 oz / 1 cup plain (all-purpose) flour
1 tsp baking powder
Pinch of salt
3 tbsp caster sugar
2 medium eggs
2 tbsp melted butter
3 tbsp elderflower syrup
300 ml / ½ pint / 1¼ cups milk

1. Chop the pecan nuts.
2. Sift the flour, baking powder and salt into a bowl and stir in the sugar. Make a well in the centre, break in the eggs and pour in the melted butter. With a whisk, gently stir the flour mixture into the eggs, gradually adding the elderflower syrup and enough of the milk to make a smooth batter the consistency of single (light) cream. Stir in the chopped pecan nuts.
3. Preheat the waffle maker to 'Medium' heat.
4. When at temperature, open the machine and pour a small ladleful of batter into the compartments, taking care not to overfill.
5. Close the machine and cook for 4–6 minutes until golden brown.
6. Cook the remaining batter, and serve warm.

Fig Pancakes with Honey

A lovely sticky filling.

Serves 4–6

4–6 ripe figs
115 g / 4 oz / 1 cup cornmeal flour
Pinch of salt
1 tbsp caster sugar
2 medium eggs
2 tbsp melted butter
300 ml / ½ pint / 1¼ cups milk
Oil or melted butter
Clear orange blossom honey, warmed

1. Cut and discard the fig stalks and cut the figs into slices from top to base.
2. Sift the cornmeal and salt into a bowl and stir in the sugar. Make a well in the centre, break in the eggs, and pour in the melted butter. With a whisk, gently stir the flour into the eggs, gradually adding enough of the milk to make a smooth batter the consistency of double (heavy) cream. If time allows, cover and leave to stand for about 15 minutes.
3. Lightly brush the crêpe maker or a non-stick frying pan with a little oil or melted butter. Preheat the crêpe maker to 'Medium', or put the non-stick frying pan over a medium heat.

4. When hot, pour a small ladleful of batter and spread to make small pancakes, about 10 cm / 4 inches across. Before the batter sets, drop 1 or 2 slices of fig onto the surface and gently push into the batter. Cook gently for about 30–45 seconds on one side until the underside is golden brown. Using a flat spatula or palette knife, carefully flip the pancake over and cook the second side for about 30–45 seconds. Lift out and keep warm.
5. Cook the remaining batter, and serve warm. Serve the pancakes with warmed honey drizzled over.

Tiramisu Pancakes

Fluffy pancakes filled with all the lovely flavours of tiramisu.

Serves 4–6

Filling
300 ml / ½ pint / 1¼ cups double (heavy) cream
200 g / 7 oz mascarpone cheese
150 ml / ¼ pint / ²/₃ cup strong black espresso coffee (cold)
2 tbsp caster sugar
3 tbsp amaretto liqueur

Pancakes
2 medium eggs
115 g / 4 oz / 1 cup plain (all-purpose) flour
Pinch of salt
1 tbsp caster sugar
1 tbsp melted butter
3 tbsp strong black espresso coffee (cold)
300 ml / ½ pint / 1¼ cups milk, less 3 tbsp
Oil or melted butter
Cocoa powder, to dust

1. Pour the cream into a bowl and whisk to soft peaks. Spoon the mascarpone cheese into a separate bowl and stir in the coffee, sugar and liqueur. Mix until smooth, then carefully fold in the whipped cream. Cover and keep cold.
2. Separate the eggs and stiffly whisk the egg whites in a grease-free bowl.

3. Sift the flour and salt into a bowl, and stir in the sugar. Make a well in the centre, add the egg yolks and pour in the melted butter. With a whisk, gently stir the flour into the eggs, gradually adding the coffee and enough of the milk to make a smooth batter the consistency of double (heavy) cream. With a spoon, fold the whisked egg whites into the batter.

4. Lightly brush the crêpe maker or a non-stick frying pan with a little oil or melted butter. Preheat the crêpe maker to 'Medium', or put the non-stick frying pan over a medium heat.

5. When hot, pour a small ladleful of batter and spread or swirl to give a thin layer. Cook gently for about 30–45 seconds on one side until the underside is golden brown. Using a flat spatula or palette knife, carefully flip the pancake over and cook the second side for about 30 seconds. Lift out and keep just warm.

6. Cook the remaining batter and serve warm.

7. Put the pancakes onto serving plates and spoon some of the tiramisu filling onto each. Dust with cocoa powder and serve immediately.

Marshmallow and Chocolate Floats

Pancakes topped with mini-marshmallows and chocolate chips – not to be eaten every day.

Makes 8–10 pancakes measuring about 10 cm / 4 inches across

55 g / 2 oz / ½ cup buckwheat flour
55 g / 2 oz / ½ cup wholemeal (whole-wheat) flour
1½ tsp baking powder
Pinch of salt
1 tbsp caster sugar
2 medium eggs
1 tsp lemon juice
2 tbsp melted butter
300 ml / ½ pint / 1¼ cups milk
Oil or melted butter
Chocolate chips
Mini marshmallows

1. Sift the buckwheat flour, wholemeal (whole-wheat) flour, baking powder and salt into a bowl and stir in the sugar. Make a well in the centre, break in the eggs, and pour in the lemon juice and melted butter. With a whisk, gently stir the flour into the eggs, gradually adding enough of the milk to make a smooth batter the consistency of double (heavy) cream. If time allows, cover and leave to stand for about 15 minutes.

2. Lightly brush the crêpe maker or a non-stick frying pan with a little oil or melted butter. Preheat the crêpe maker to 'Medium', or put the non-stick frying pan over a medium heat.

3. When hot, pour a small ladleful of batter and spread to make pancakes about 7.5 cm / 3 inches across. Cook gently for about 30–45 seconds on one side until the underside is golden brown. Using a flat spatula or palette knife, carefully flip the pancake over and scatter a few chocolate chips and marshmallows on the cooked pancake. They will soften and melt a little while the second side cooks, about 30–45 seconds. Lift out and keep warm.
4. Cook the remaining batter, and serve warm.

Chocolate Pancake Stack

Definitely one for special occasions – opulent and decadent.

Serves 4–6

Filling
200 g / 7 oz plain chocolate
200 ml / 7 fl oz cream
140 g / 5 oz peanut brittle
4 tbsp apricot conserve

Pancakes
115 g / 4 oz / 1 cup plain (all-purpose) flour, less 2 tbsp
2 tbsp cocoa powder
Pinch of salt
2 medium eggs
1 tbsp melted butter
300 ml / ½ pint / 1¼ cups milk
Oil or melted butter

1. Break the chocolate into a microwave-proof bowl and pour over the cream. Heat in a microwave oven on a low power setting for a few seconds at a time until the chocolate has melted and the cream is hot. Beat until smooth and leave to cool.
2. Put the peanut brittle into a food (freezer) bag and tap the brittle until crushed.
3. Sift the plain (all-purpose) flour, cocoa powder and salt into a bowl. Make a well in the centre, break in the eggs and pour in the melted butter. With a whisk, gently stir the flour into the eggs, gradually adding enough of the milk to make a smooth batter the consistency of single (light) cream. If time allows, cover and leave to stand for about 30 minutes.

4. Lightly brush the crêpe maker or a non-stick frying pan with a little oil or melted butter. Preheat the crêpe maker to 'Medium', or put the non-stick frying pan over a medium heat.

5. When hot, pour a small ladleful of batter and spread or swirl to give a thin layer. Cook gently for about 30–45 seconds on one side until the underside is golden brown. Using a flat spatula or palette knife, carefully flip the pancake over and cook the second side for about 30 seconds. Lift out.

6. Cook the remaining batter, making about 8–10 pancakes in total. Put a pancake on a plate and thinly spread with apricot conserve and some of the chocolate mixture. Sprinkle over crushed peanut brittle and top with another pancake. Repeat until the pancakes are in a stack. Serve cold, cut into wedges.

Fruit Salad Pancakes

Like open fruit tarts, these pancakes have a luscious fruit topping. Serve with cream or maple syrup.

Serves 4–6

250 g / 9 oz small, mixed fruits, blueberries, grapes, blackcurrants, raspberries
115 g / 4 oz / 1 cup self-raising (self-rising) flour
Pinch of salt
1 tbsp caster sugar
2 medium eggs
¼ tsp vanilla extract
1 tbsp melted butter
300 ml / ½ pint / 1¼ cups milk
Oil or melted butter

1. Cut in half any larger fruits, such as grapes. Sift the flour and salt into a bowl and stir in the sugar. Make a well in the centre and break in the eggs, vanilla extract and melted butter. With a whisk, gently stir the flour into the eggs, gradually adding the milk to make a smooth batter the consistency of single (light) cream. If time allows,

cover and leave to stand for about 15 minutes.

2. Lightly brush the crêpe maker or a non-stick frying pan with a little oil or melted butter. Preheat the crêpe maker to 'Medium', or put the non-stick frying pan over a medium heat.

3. When hot, pour a small ladleful of batter and spread or swirl to give a thin layer. Scatter a little of the mixed fruits over the top. Cook gently for about 30–45 seconds on one side until the underside is golden brown. Using a flat spatula or palette knife, carefully flip the pancake over and cook the second side for about 30 seconds, taking care not to let the fruits brown too much. Lift out and keep warm.

4. Cook the remaining batter, and serve warm.

Sour Cherry and Sesame Seed Waffles

Sour cherries bursting with flavour and crunchy sesame seeds.

Makes about 8–10 waffles

60 g / 2¼ oz dried, ready-to-eat sour cherries
115 g / 4 oz / 1 cup plain (all-purpose) flour
1 tsp baking powder
Pinch of salt
3 tbsp caster sugar
2 medium eggs
2 tbsp melted butter
300 ml / ½ pint / 1¼ cups milk
2 tbsp sesame seeds

1. Cut the sour cherries in half.
2. Sift the flour, baking powder and salt into a bowl and stir in the sugar. Make a well in the centre, break in the eggs and pour in the melted butter. With a whisk, gently stir the flour mixture into the eggs, gradually adding enough of the milk to make a smooth batter the consistency of single (light) cream. Stir in the sour cherries and sesame seeds.
3. Preheat the waffle maker to 'Medium' heat.
4. When at temperature, open the machine and pour a small ladleful of batter into the compartments, taking care not to overfill.
5. Close the machine and cook for 4–6 minutes until golden brown.
6. Cook the remaining batter, making about 8–10 waffles in total, and serve warm.

Oven-Baked
Filled Pancakes

MOST OF THESE RECIPES (where indicated) start with the recipe for a basic pancakes, which can be found on page 16. If you prefer, or to save time, you can always use shop-bought, ready-made pancakes as a starting point for these dishes, or home-made pancakes from your freezer.

So the recipes generally start the same, but they go off in unpredictable directions. Some of the pancakes get rolled and filled, some get cut into shapes, and some will end up transformed, into a pizza, an asparagus tart or a cheesecake.

The flavours and ingredients are rich and diverse, savoury or sweet, hearty or delicate, but all of these pancakes are alike in going into the oven to be baked. You then have an appetizing wait (not too long) before the baked pancake dishes emerge, piping hot and ready to be devoured.

Some of the recipes in this chapter have lots of stages to them. You can often shorten the process by preparing sauces in advance or by taking a jar from your store-cupboard or pantry.

Sausage Breakfast in a Pancake

Breakfast in a pancake. You may want to add a rasher (strip) or two of bacon.

Serves 4

8 plain pancakes 18 cm / 7 inches across (page 16)

Filling
5 tomatoes
6 button mushrooms
2 tsp oil
8 thick butcher's sausages, your favourite
175 g / 6 oz light cream cheese
Tomato ketchup or brown sauce
40 g / 1½ oz grated Cheddar cheese or other hard cheese

1. Preheat the oven to 200°C, Fan 185°C, 400°F, Gas 6.
2. Thinly slice the tomatoes and the mushrooms.
3. Heat the oil in a pan and fry the sausages until browned and cooked through. Add the mushroom slices 5 minutes before the end and stir until cooked.
4. Spread some cream cheese over each pancake. Arrange a few mushroom and tomato slices along one edge. Top with a sausage, and spoon or squirt tomato ketchup or brown sauce over the sausage.
5. Roll the pancakes over the filling and lift into an ovenproof dish, arranging them in a single layer. Scatter over the grated cheese.
6. Cover with foil and put into the hot oven. Cook for 15 minutes, remove the foil and cook for a further 10 minutes until golden and piping hot.

Chicken Curry Pancakes

An easy dish, made with handy spices and pastes. Use different curry pastes to completely change the flavour. Serve with salad, chutneys and pickles.

Serves 4

8 plain thin pancakes about 18 cm / 7 inches across (page 16)

Filling
Small bunch coriander (cilantro) leaves
4 spring onions (scallions)
Small piece fresh ginger
3 cooked, roasted, chicken breasts
150 ml / ¼ pint / ²/₃ cup pint thick natural yogurt
150 ml / ¼ pint / ²/₃ cup coconut milk
2 tsp liquid chicken stock
1 tbsp mild / medium-hot curry paste, your favourite
Freshly milled salt and pepper

Topping
2 tbsp melted butter
1–2 tbsp sesame seeds

1. Preheat the oven to 200°C, Fan 185°C, 400°F, Gas 6.
2. Pull the coriander (cilantro) leaves from the stalks and finely chop. Thinly slice the spring onions and grate the ginger. Remove any skin from the chicken breasts and slice or tear into long thin pieces.
3. Pour the yogurt and coconut milk into a large bowl and stir in the liquid stock and curry paste. Add the chopped coriander (cilantro), sliced spring onions (scallions) and grated ginger. Season with salt and pepper, if necessary.

4. Put the strips of chicken on one side of the pancakes and spoon over the yogurt mixture.
5. Roll the pancakes over the filling and lift into an ovenproof dish, arranging them in a single layer. Brush or drizzle with melted butter and sprinkle over the sesame seeds.
6. Cover with foil and put into the hot oven. Cook for 15 minutes, remove the foil and cook for a further 10 minutes until golden and piping hot.

Smoked Haddock Pancakes

There are several steps to this dish, including cooking the fish and making the sauce, but the end result is very tasty. Use a coil whisk or balloon whisk to mix 'all-in-one' sauces – they will always be smooth. Serve with lemon wedges to squeeze over.

Serves 4

8 plain pancakes 18 cm / 7 inches across (page 16)

Filling
350 g / 12 oz smoked haddock
300 ml / ½ pint / 1¼ cups milk, plus extra
1 bay leaf
Freshly milled black pepper and salt
2 rashers (strips) streaky bacon
25 g / 1 oz plain flour
25 g / 1 oz butter
1 tsp wholegrain mustard
1 tbsp chopped parsley
3 tbsp peas

1. Preheat the oven to 190°C, Fan 175°C, 375°F, Gas 5.
2. Put the haddock into a pan, pour over half of the milk. Add the bay leaf and a little black pepper. Cover, and cook over a gentle heat for 5–8 minutes until the fish starts to flake. Grill (broil) the bacon rashers (strips) until crisp and golden.
3. Drain the haddock, reserving any liquid. Flake the fish and put into a bowl. Cut the bacon into small pieces and add to the flaked fish.

4. Measure the reserved liquid and make up to 300 ml / ½ pint / 1¼ cups with extra milk. Pour into a pan and add the flour, butter and mustard. Gently heat and bring to the boil, stirring all the time. Cook for 2–3 minutes. Remove from the heat and stir in the parsley, peas and, if necessary, season with a little salt and pepper.

5. Spread the haddock and bacon mixture over the pancakes.

6. Roll the pancakes over the filling and lift into an ovenproof dish, arranging them in a single layer.

7. Cover with foil and put into the hot oven. Cook for 30–35 minutes until golden and piping hot.

Parcelled Prawns (Shrimps)

There's an oriental taste to this filling. It also works well with mixed shellfish, salmon or trout.

Serves 2

4 plain thin pancakes about 18 cm / 7 inches across (page 16)

Filling
6 cherry tomatoes
Small handful rocket (arugula) leaves
6 cos lettuce leaves, or other crisp leaves
2 spring onions (scallions)
1 tsp garlic purée
1 tsp light soy sauce
1 tsp rice wine vinegar
Freshly milled salt and black pepper
250g / 9 oz cooked prawns (shrimps)

Topping
2 tsp oil
2 tbsp chopped almonds
3 tbsp grated Parmesan cheese

1. Preheat the oven to 200°C, Fan 185°C, 400°F, Gas 6.
2. Chop the cherry tomatoes. Finely shred the rocket (arugula) leaves, cos lettuce leaves and spring onions (scallions). Mix all together in a bowl.
3. In a bowl, spoon the garlic purée, soy sauce, rice wine vinegar, and a little seasoning. Mix and stir in the cooked prawns (shrimps). If there's time, cover the prawn (shrimp) mixture and leave for 15 minutes for the flavours to develop.

4. Put some of the tomato mix in the centre of each pancake and top with a spoonful of the prawn (shrimp) mixture. Fold two opposite sides into the centre and fold the other two sides over to make a parcel. Turn them over, seam-side down, and gently press to neaten the shape.
5. Lift them onto a baking sheet and brush with a little oil. In a small bowl, mix together the almonds and Parmesan cheese.
6. Put into the hot oven and cook for 12–18 minutes until piping hot and cooked through. Cover with foil if they brown too much.

Pancake Pizzas

Keep a stash of these yeasted pizzas in the freezer. The topping quantities I've given here are for four pizzas. But just increase or decrease the amount to serve ten or just one. Vary the ingredients to suit – in place of the salami, try cooked turkey or chicken.

Serves 4

Pancakes
115 g / 4 oz / 1 cup plain (all-purpose) flour
Pinch of salt
1 tsp caster sugar
½ tsp fast-action dried yeast
2 medium eggs
1 tbsp olive oil
300 ml / ½ pint / 1¼ cups milk
Oil or melted butter

Topping for 4 pizzas
1 small red onion
4 cherry tomatoes
Few sprigs of fresh oregano
Small handful of spinach leaves
140 g / 5 oz mozzarella cheese
60 g / 2¼ oz Cheddar cheese
8 pitted black olives
150 ml / ¼ pint / about ⅔ cup passata (sieved tomatoes)
1 tbsp tomato purée
8 salami slices
1 tbsp olive oil

1. Sift the flour and salt into a bowl and add the sugar. Stir in the yeast. Make a well in the centre and break in the eggs and pour in the oil. With a whisk, gently stir the flour into the eggs, gradually adding enough of the milk to make a smooth batter the consistency of double (heavy) cream. Cover the bowl with oiled clear film (plastic wrap) and leave in a warm place until doubled in size, about 45 minutes to an hour. Before using, mix the batter and, if too thick, stir in a little milk.

2. Lightly brush the crêpe maker or a non-stick frying pan with a little oil or melted butter. Preheat the crêpe maker to 'Medium', or put the non-stick frying pan over a medium heat.

3. When hot, pour in and spread sufficient batter to give a pancake measuring about 15 cm / 6 inches across. Cook gently for about 30–45 seconds on one side until the underside is golden brown. Using a flat spatula or palette knife, carefully flip the pancake over and cook the second side for about 30 seconds. Lift out and cook the remaining batter. Use 4 pancakes for this recipe and freeze the rest.

4. Heat the oven to 190°C, Fan 175°C, 375° F, Gas 5.

5. Make the pizza topping. Thinly slice the onion and slice the tomatoes. Pull the leaves from the oregano sprigs and, if large, tear the spinach leaves into small pieces.

6. Tear the mozzarella cheese into small pieces and coarsely grate the Cheddar cheese. Slice the olives. In a small bowl, mix the passata with the tomato purée. Roughly chop the salami.

7. Put 4 pancakes onto baking sheets. Spread the tomato mixture almost to the edges and scatter the spinach leaves over. Arrange the onion slices, tomato slices and salami on top. Scatter over oregano leaves, olive slices and mozzarella and Cheddar cheeses. Drizzle with the oil.

8. Put into the hot oven and cook for 12–15 minutes until the topping is golden brown and cooked through.

Hot Lamb and Tomato Pancake Stack

Serve with green beans or broccoli. The meat sauce freezes well, so double up the recipe for the filling and keep some in reserve.

Serves 4

8 plain pancakes about 18 cm / 7 inches across (page 16)

Filling
1 red onion
1 garlic clove
Small bunch of coriander (cilantro)
1 tbsp oil
350 g / 12 oz lean, minced lamb
400 g / 14 oz can chopped tomatoes
3 tsp liquid vegetable stock
1 tsp chilli paste
Pinch sugar
Freshly milled salt and black pepper
70 g / 2½ oz grated Gruyère cheese

1. Finely chop the red onion and crush the garlic. Pull the coriander (cilantro) leaves from the stalks and finely chop.

2. Heat the oil in a pan and fry the onion until softened. Stir in the minced lamb and cook for 5 minutes. Tip in the can of tomatoes, crushed garlic, vegetable stock, chilli paste, sugar and half of the chopped coriander (cilantro). Cover the pan and cook for 20–30 minutes until quite thick and cooked through. Halfway through cooking, preheat the oven to 190°C, Fan 175°C, 375°F, Gas 5. Stir in the remaining chopped coriander (cilantro). Season, if necessary, with a little salt and pepper.

3. Put one pancake into a wide ovenproof dish and spoon over some of the tomato mixture, spreading it almost to the edges. Scatter over a little grated cheese and top with another pancake. Repeat until all the pancakes are used.

4. Cover the dish with foil and put into the hot oven. If the sauce is used when freshly made and hot, then cook for 20 minutes. If the sauce is cold when used, then cook for 40–45 minutes until piping hot throughout.

5. Cut into wedges to serve.

Asparagus Pancake Tarts

In place of pastry, I've used a thin pancake as the 'case' for the filling. Serve with salad and a glass of wine.

Makes 6

6 plain thin pancakes 10 cm / 4 inches across (page 16)
Oil for greasing

Filling
Small bunch of chives
12 cooked asparagus spears
3 medium eggs
300 ml / ½ pint / 1¼ cups milk
Freshly milled salt and pepper
3 tbsp peas
3 tbsp sweetcorn
5 tbsp grated Gruyère cheese

1. Preheat the oven to 180°C, Fan 165°C, 350°F, Gas 4. Lightly grease six 10 cm / 4 inch deep tartlet or muffin tins.
2. With scissors, finely snip the chives. Cut each asparagus spear into three. Break the eggs into a bowl, lightly beat and stir in the milk and the chives. Season lightly with salt and pepper.

3. Fold and shape each pancake to fit into each tartlet or muffin tin. The pancakes will sit above the level of the tins.
4. Spoon some of the asparagus, peas and sweetcorn into each pancake case.
5. Pour over the egg mixture and sprinkle over the cheese.
6. Put into the hot oven and bake for 20–30 minutes until golden and cooked through.

Crisp Pancake Triangles

Great as snacks, or to nibble with drinks. The topping is quick to whiz with a food processor, but of course you can also just chop the ingredients finely. Use a pancake maker or a pan to dry torn pieces of pancake for a few seconds on either side, so they are ready to dunk into dips.

Serves 6–8

6 plain pancakes 10 cm / 4 inches across (page 16)

Topping
1 red chilli (page 8)
3 spring onions (scallions)
Small piece of fresh ginger
Small bunch of parsley
2 garlic cloves
2 tbsp olive oil
2 tbsp tomato purée
3 tbsp Parmesan cheese
Freshly milled salt and pepper

1. Preheat the oven to 180°C, Fan 165°C, 350°F, Gas 4.
2. Cut the chilli in half, remove and discard the seeds and stalk. Cut the spring onions (scallions) into three. Peel or scrape the ginger. Pull the leaves off the parsley sprigs.

3. Put the chilli, spring onions (scallions) and ginger into a food processor. Process for a few seconds until coarsely chopped. Add the parsley leaves, garlic cloves, oil, tomato purée and Parmesan cheese. Process again for a few seconds until finely chopped, but not a paste. Taste and season, if necessary, with salt or pepper.

4. Cut each pancake into quarters and spread with a very thin layer of the topping. Lift onto baking sheets.

5. Put into the hot oven and cook for 10–15 minutes until the pancake triangles have dried and started to crisp. Serve hot or cold.

Spinach and Cheese Pancakes

(as shown on the front cover)

Very simple ingredients, but what flavour! Replace the spinach with rocket (arugula), or go half and half. Rocket (arugula) will add a peppery taste to the dish.

Serves 4

8 plain pancakes 18 cm / 7 inches across (page 16)

Filling
2 large handfuls of small spinach leaves
40 g / 1½ oz Cheddar cheese or other hard cheese
3 tbsp chopped toasted hazelnuts
450 ml / ¾ pint / about 2 cups cheese sauce

1. Preheat the oven to 190°C, Fan 175°C, 375°F, Gas 5.
2. Put the spinach leaves into a pan with a few tbsp cold water. Heat and cook for 1–2 minutes until wilted.
3. Rinse under cold water, then drain and squeeze out any excess water.
4. Coarsely grate the cheese. Stir half of the chopped hazelnuts into the sauce.

5. Spread a little cheese sauce over each pancake (reserving one third). Cover each pancake with a few spinach leaves.
6. Roll the pancakes over the filling and lift into an ovenproof dish, arranging them in a single layer. Pour over the remaining sauce and scatter over the remaining hazelnuts.
7. Cover with foil and put into the hot oven. Cook for 10 minutes, remove the foil and cook for a further 10–15 minutes until golden and piping hot.

Bananas, Grapes and Custard Filled Pancakes

Always a favourite, invoking memories from childhood. I've added some grapes, but try raspberries or blueberries.

Serves 4

4 thin sweet pancakes 18 cm / 7 inches across (page 16)

Filling
4 bananas
Small handful seedless green grapes
150 ml / ¼ pint / generous ⅔ cup prepared English custard
4–6 tbsp plum conserve
Icing sugar, to dust

1. Preheat the oven to 200°C, Fan 185°C, 400°F, Gas 6.
2. Thinly slice the bananas. Cut the grapes into quarters.
3. Pour the custard into a bowl and stir in the sliced bananas and grapes.
4. Spread some plum conserve over each pancake. Spoon some of the custard mixture onto one half of each pancake. Roll the pancakes over the filling and lift into an ovenproof dish, arranging them in a single layer.
5. Cover with foil and put into the hot oven. Cook for 15–20 minutes until piping hot and cooked through
6. Dust with icing sugar and serve immediately.

Coconut, Pineapple and Ricotta Pancakes

The pineapple slices can be fresh or canned in natural juice.

Serves 4

4 thin sweet pancakes about 18 cm / 7 inches across (page 16)

Filling
5 pineapple slices
175 g / 6 oz ricotta cheese
1 tsp ground cinnamon
1 tbsp rum or orange juice
5 tbsp desiccated coconut
1 tbsp melted butter

1. Preheat the oven to 200°C, Fan 185°C, 400°F, Gas 6.
2. Finely chop the pineapple slices.
3. Pour the ricotta cheese into a bowl and stir in the ground cinnamon and the rum or orange juice. Mix until smooth and stir in half of the desiccated coconut and the pineapple pieces.
4. Spoon and spread some of the pineapple mixture over each pancake. Roll the pancakes over the filling and lift into an ovenproof dish, arranging them in a single layer.
5. Brush with a little melted butter and sprinkle over the remaining coconut.
6. Cover with foil and put into the hot oven. Cook for 15 minutes, remove the foil and cook for a further 5 minutes until golden brown hot and cooked through.

Pancake Raisin Cheesecakes

Pancakes into cheesecakes – the pancakes becoming the 'pastry cases'.

Makes 6

6 thin sweet pancakes 10 cm / 4 inches across (page 16)
Oil for greasing

Filling
1 lime
3 medium eggs
175 g / 6 oz light cream cheese
4 tbsp milk
¼ tsp ground nutmeg
175 g / 6 oz raisins
Icing sugar, to dust

1. Preheat the oven to 180°C, Fan 165°C, 350°F, Gas 4. Lightly grease six 10 cm / 4 inch deep tartlet or muffin tins.
2. Finely grate the rind from the lime. Cut in half and squeeze out the juice.
3. Break the eggs into a bowl, lightly beat and stir in the cream cheese, milk, nutmeg, lime rind and juice. Thoroughly mix until smooth then stir in the raisins.
4. Fold and shape each pancake to fit into each tartlet or muffin tin. The pancakes will sit above the level of the tins.
5. Spoon some of the filling into each pancake case and level the surface.
6. Put into the hot oven and bake for 25–35 minutes until the filling is firm to the touch. Cover with foil if the top becomes too brown.
7. Leave to cool and dust with icing sugar before serving.

Pancakes with Strawberries and Cream

Strawberries and cream, with a little maple syrup and a hint of mint – divine.

Serves 4

4 thin sweet pancakes about 18 cm / 7 inches across (page 16)

Filling
250 g / 9 oz small strawberries
125 ml / ¼ pint / generous ²/₃ cup double (heavy) cream
2 tbsp maple syrup
4 mint leaves

1. Preheat the oven to 200°C, Fan 185°C, 400°F, Gas 6.
2. Quarter the strawberries (if using frozen, drain off any excess liquid). Pour the cream into a bowl and lightly whisk.
3. Spread a little cream over each pancake. Scatter over the strawberry pieces and drizzle over some maple syrup. Put a mint leaf in the middle of each pancake.
4. Roll the pancakes over the filling and lift into an ovenproof dish, arranging them in a single layer.
5. Cover with foil and put into the hot oven. Cook for 15 minutes, remove the foil and cook for a further 5 minutes until cooked through.

Pancakes with Roasted Plums

There are a few steps to this recipe, with the plums being roasted beforehand. The filling will keep in the fridge for two days. In place of the plums, try roasted peaches or nectarine slices.

Serves 4

4 thin sweet pancakes about 18 cm / 7 inches across (page 16)

Filling
1 lime
10 ripe plums
1 tbsp melted butter
2 tbsp soft brown sugar
175 g / 6 oz soured cream
4 tbsp salted peanuts

1. To roast the plums, preheat the oven to 200°C, Fan 185°C, 400°F, Gas 6.
2. Finely grate the rind from half the lime, cut in half and squeeze out the juice. Cut around the plum stones (pits), twist and remove the stones (pits) with a sharp knife. Cut each piece in half again.
3. Put the plum quarters into a small ovenproof dish, pour over the melted butter, lime rind and juice and sprinkle over the sugar.
4. Put into the hot oven and cook for 15–20 minutes, turning once until cooked and beginning to brown. Chill until cold.
5. To complete the dish, preheat the oven (as above). Spoon some of the cold plums onto each pancake. Add a blob of soured cream. Spoon over any syrup from the plums and scatter over the peanuts.

6. Fold the pancakes over the filling and lift into an ovenproof dish, arranging them in a single layer.
7. Put into the hot oven and cook for 15 minutes until piping hot and cooked through.

Meringue-topped Apricot Pancakes

Filled pancakes smothered in a soft meringue.

Serves 4

4 thin sweet pancakes about 18 cm / 7 inches across (page 16)

Filling
8 apricots
4 tbsp apricot conserve
4 tbsp natural yogurt
2 medium egg whites
3 tbsp icing sugar
Icing sugar, to dredge

1. Preheat the oven to 190°C, Fan 175°C, 375°F, Gas 5.
2. Cut the apricots in half, remove the stones (pits) and thinly slice.
3. Spoon the conserve into a bowl, pour in the yogurt and mix thoroughly.
4. Spread the yogurt mixture over the pancakes and scatter over the sliced apricots.
5. Roll the pancakes over the filling and arrange next to each other in an ovenproof dish.
6. In a grease-free bowl, whisk the egg whites until very stiff and fold in the icing sugar. Spoon and swirl the meringue over the pancakes.
7. Put into the hot oven and cook for 20–25 minutes until golden and set. Dredge with icing sugar.

Pancakes with Dried Figs and Apricots

Sticky and chewy.

Serves 4

4 thin sweet pancakes about 18 cm / 7 inches across (page 16)

Filling
3 dried, ready-to-eat-figs or prunes
3 dried, ready-to-eat apricots
8 glacé cherries
1 eating apple
1 tsp ground allspice
2 tbsp soft brown sugar
175 g / 6 oz cottage cheese

1. Preheat the oven to 200°C, Fan 185°C, 400°F, Gas 6.
2. Finely chop the prunes, apricots and glacé cherries and put into a small bowl.
3. Peel, core and finely chop the apple and stir into the dried fruit mixture.
4. Stir in the ground allspice, brown sugar and cottage cheese and mix well.
5. Spoon some of the fruit mixture over each pancake. Roll the pancakes over the filling and lift into an ovenproof dish, arranging them in a single layer.
6. Cover with foil and put into the hot oven. Cook for 15–20 minutes, remove the foil and cook for a further 5 minutes until golden brown, hot and cooked through.

Chocolate, Ginger and Hazelnut Pancake Rolls

Delicious hot or cold. When cold cut into thin slices. Not for the faint-hearted.

Serves 4–8

8 thin sweet pancakes about 10 cm / 4 inches across (page 16)

Filling
8 ginger biscuits (cookies)
100 g / 3½ oz 70% plain chocolate
100 g / 3½ oz chopped, toasted hazelnuts
2 tbsp rum, or orange juice
2–3 tbsp milk
Cocoa powder, to dust

1. Preheat the oven to 200°C, Fan 185°C, 400°F, Gas 6.
2. Put the biscuits (cookies) into a food (freezer) bag and tap with a rolling pin until finely crushed.
3. Break the chocolate into a microwave-proof bowl and heat on a low power setting for a few seconds until melted, or on the hob over a pan of hot water, but don't let the base of the bowl sit in the water.

4. Tip the crushed biscuits (cookies) into the bowl of melted chocolate and stir in the chopped hazelnuts and the rum or orange juice. Mix thoroughly and stir in a little milk to give a spreading consistency.
5. Spoon and spread a little of the mixture over each pancake. Roll the pancakes over the filling and lift into an ovenproof dish, arranging them in a single layer.
6. Cover with foil and put into the hot oven. Cook for 8 minutes, remove the foil and cook for a further 2–3 minutes until piping hot. Dust with cocoa powder.

Apple, Walnut and Honey Parcels

Very, very rich and sticky. If you are making the pancakes from scratch for this recipe, don't let them colour too much. Serve with yogurt.

Serves 4

4 thin sweet pancakes about 18 cm / 7 inches across (page 16)

Filling
2 small eating apples
2 tsp lemon juice
10 walnut halves
4 tbsp clear honey
1 tsp ground cinnamon
2 tbsp melted butter
Icing sugar, to dredge

1. Preheat the oven to 200°C, Fan 185°C, 400°F, Gas 6.
2. Peel, core and grate the apples into a bowl. Stir in the lemon juice. Roughly chop the walnuts.
3. Spoon the honey into the grated apple and mix in the cinnamon and chopped walnuts.
4. Put a spoonful of the walnut mixture in the centre of each pancake. Fold two opposite sides into the centre and fold the other two sides over to make a parcel. Turn them over, seam-side down, and gently press to neaten the shape.
5. Lift them onto a baking sheet and brush with the melted butter.
6. Put into the hot oven and cook for 10–15 minutes until piping hot and cooked through. Cover with foil if they brown too much. Dredge with icing sugar as soon as they come out of the oven.

7

Toppings to Spoon, Drizzle or Spread

THIS CHAPTER encourages you to spoon, drizzle and spread. In other words, try your hand at these ideal methods of decking out your waffles and pancakes.

There are plenty of snappy, snazzy ideas. Some of these toppings are old favourites, others combine flavours in a more contemporary way. All are quick and simple to make, and well worth a go.

Spicy Curry

Serves 4, can be halved or doubled

- In a saucepan, fry 450 g / 1 lb / 4 cups lean minced beef, chicken or lamb in a little oil with 1 finely chopped onion and 1 finely chopped carrot. Cook for 8 minutes. Stir in 1–3 tsp medium-hot curry paste (choose your favourite), 1 tsp garlic purée, 1 red (bell) pepper, halved, stalk and seeds removed, and finely chopped, 400 g / 14 oz can of chopped tomatoes, 300 ml / ½ pint / 1¼ cups vegetable stock, freshly milled salt and black pepper. Bring just to the boil, reduce the heat and cook for 35 minutes until piping hot and cooked through. Stir in 2 tbsp chopped parsley just before serving.

Hot Chilli

Serves 4, can be halved or doubled

- In a saucepan, fry 450 g / 1 lb / 4 cups lean minced beef, chicken or lamb in a little oil with 1 finely chopped onion and 1 finely chopped carrot. Cook for 8 minutes. Stir in ¼ tsp hot paprika pepper, ½ tsp ground cumin, 1 tsp garlic purée, 1 tsp chilli paste, 1 red (bell) pepper, halved, stalk and seeds removed, and finely chopped, 400 g / 14 oz can of chopped tomatoes, 300 ml / ½ pint / 1¼ cups vegetable stock, freshly milled salt and black pepper. Bring just to the boil, reduce the heat and cook for 35 minutes until piping hot and cooked through. Stir in 2 tbsp chopped parsley just before serving.

Olive and Lemon Tajine

Serves 4, can be halved or doubled

- In a saucepan, fry 450 g / 1 lb / 4 cups lean minced beef, chicken or lamb in a little oil with 1 finely chopped onion and 1 finely chopped carrot. Cook for 8 minutes. Stir in ½ tsp ground turmeric, 1 tsp caraway seeds, 2 tsp garlic purée, 1 red (bell) pepper, halved, stalk and seeds removed, and finely chopped, rind and juice of a lemon, 400 g / 14 oz can of chopped tomatoes, 300 ml / ½ pint / 1¼ cups vegetable stock, freshly milled salt and black pepper. Bring just to the boil, reduce the heat and cook for 35 minutes until piping hot and cooked through. After 25 minutes' cooking, stir in 12 green or black pitted olives and 2 tbsp chopped parsley.

Mustard Sausages

Serves 4, can be halved or doubled

- In a saucepan, fry 450 g / 1 lb of your favourite sausages, each cut into 4, in a little oil with 1 finely chopped onion and 1 finely chopped carrot. Cook for 8 minutes. Stir in 2 tbsp wholegrain mustard, 2 tbsp mango chutney, 1 tsp garlic purée, 1 red (bell) pepper, halved, stalk and seeds removed, and finely chopped, 400 g / 14 oz can of chopped tomatoes, 300 ml / ½ pint / 1¼ cups vegetable stock, freshly milled salt and black pepper. Bring just to the boil, reduce the heat and cook for 35 minutes until piping hot and cooked through. Stir in 2 tbsp chopped parsley just before serving.

Thai Fish

Serves 4, can be halved or doubled

- In a saucepan, fry 1 finely chopped onion and 6 sliced mushrooms in a little oil for 6 minutes. Stir in 1 tbsp green Thai curry paste, 1 tsp lemon grass purée, 1 tsp garlic purée, 1 red (bell) pepper, halved, stalk and seeds removed, and finely chopped, 400 g / 14 oz can of chopped tomatoes, 150 ml / ¼ pint / ^{2}/$_3$ cup coconut milk, 150 ml / ¼ pint / ^{2}/$_3$ cup vegetable stock, freshly milled salt and pepper. Bring just to the boil, reduce the heat and cook for 10 minutes. Stir in 450 g / 1 lb skinned, boneless, chopped fish pieces, a large handful of spinach leaves and 2 tbsp chopped parsley. Cook for a further 10 minutes until piping hot and cooked through.

Vegetables with Pine Nuts and Sesame Seeds

Serves 4, can be halved or doubled

- In a saucepan, fry 450 g / 1 lb / 6 cups shredded vegetables (such as courgette (zucchini), aubergine (eggplant), fennel bulb and carrot) in a little oil with 1 very finely chopped onion. Cook for 4–6 minutes, stirring a few times. Stir in a grated 1 cm / ½ inch piece of root ginger, 1 tsp garlic purée, 1 tsp chilli paste, 1 red (bell) pepper, halved, stalk and seeds removed, and finely chopped, 400 g / 14 oz can of chopped tomatoes, 300 ml / ½ pint / 1¼ cups vegetable stock, freshly milled salt and black pepper. Bring just to the boil, reduce the heat and cook for 15 minutes. Stir in 2 tbsp chopped parsley, 2 tbsp toasted sesame seeds and a handful of pine nuts. Cook for a further 10 minutes until piping hot and cooked through.

Citrus Strands

- Cut a lemon, an orange and a lime in half and squeeze out the juices into a pan. With a sharp knife, cut each piece of fruit skin into four wedges. Scrape off as much of the white pith as possible and cut into thin strips. Pour 6 tbsp of caster sugar over the fruit juice and add 150 ml / ¼ pint / ²/₃ cup boiling water (from a kettle). Stir until the sugar has melted, bring to the boil and boil rapidly for 5 minutes. Add the strips of fruit rind and cook for 10 minutes or until soft, but not falling apart. Leave until cold then spoon into a bowl, cover and chill.

Blueberries in Vodka

- Fill a sterilized bottle with blueberries (each one pierced with a fine skewer). Add sugar to come halfway up the bottle and pour in vodka to fill. Put the lid on and shake the bottle every day for two weeks, topping up the bottle with vodka as the sugar dissolves. Put in a dark cupboard for a few weeks. Spoon a few blueberries onto hot crêpes or waffles with ice cream or yogurt. Try with gin or brandy in place of the vodka.

Mascarpone and Orange Cream

- Spoon 175 g / 6 oz / 1 cup mascarpone cheese into a bowl. Stir in 60 g / 2¼ oz sifted icing sugar and the rind and juice of an orange. Mix thoroughly and stir in 150 ml / ¼ pint / $^2/_3$ cup single (light) or double (heavy) cream. Cover and chill.

Chocolate Sauce

A simple recipe to make – use equal quantities of chocolate and double (heavy) cream, such as 200 g / 7 oz chocolate and 200 ml / 7 fl oz cream.

- Break the chocolate into a bowl and pour over the cream. Then heat in a microwave on a low power setting for a few seconds at a time until the chocolate has melted and the cream is hot. Alternatively, put the bowl over a pan of hot water on the hob and heat until hot (the bowl must be clear of the water). Beat until smooth.

Flavoured Butters

Serves 6–8

Useful to keep in the fridge. Spread onto hot waffles or pancakes. To pour or drizzle, gently heat in the microwave for a few seconds on a low power level.

- Put 115 g / 4 oz / ½ cup butter (or unsalted butter if making a sweet version) into a bowl and mix until soft (or soften in the microwave on a low power level). Carefully stir in your savoury or sweet ingredients selection and season with a little freshly milled salt and pepper, or sweeten with a little sieved icing sugar or clear honey. Spoon into small dishes, cover and chill until needed, or freeze. Low-fat spreads can also be used, but the flavour won't be the same.

Savoury Butters

To the softened butter, add one of the following selections:

Parsley, Lemon and Spring Onion (Scallion)
- 1 tbsp finely chopped parsley, 1 tsp grated lemon rind and a finely chopped spring onion (scallion).

Basil and Chive
- A small handful of torn basil leaves and finely chopped chives.

Chilli and Coriander (Cilantro)
- ½–1 tsp chilli paste and 3 tbsp chopped coriander (cilantro).

Mustard and Honey
- 2 tbsp wholegrain mustard and 1 tsp clear honey.

Sweet Versions

To the softened unsalted butter, add one of the following selections:

Lime and Ginger
- 1 tsp grated lime rind and 1 tbsp finely chopped crystallized ginger.

Orange and Almond
- ¼ tsp finely grated orange rind and 2 tbsp chopped toasted almonds.

Cherry Conserve and Lemon
- 3 tbsp cherry conserve and ½ tsp lemon juice.

Honey and Spice
- 2 tbsp clear honey and ¼ tsp ground cinnamon.

Yogurt or Cream

Serves 6–8

Useful to keep in the fridge. Serve with hot waffles, or plain or filled pancakes. Serve warm or cold. Gently heat in the microwave for a few seconds on a low power level.

- Pour 300 ml / ½ pint / 1¼ cups thick natural yogurt or double (heavy) cream into a bowl. Carefully stir in your savoury or sweet ingredients selection and season with a little freshly milled salt and pepper, or sweeten with a little sieved icing sugar or clear honey. Stir in a little milk if the mixture is too thick. Spoon into jugs, cover and chill until needed. In the sweet versions, English custard can replace the yogurt or cream.

Savoury Versions

To the yogurt or double (heavy) cream, add one of the following selections:

Coconut and Coriander (Cilantro)
- Replace half of the yogurt or cream with coconut milk and stir in 3 tbsp chopped coriander (cilantro) leaves, a pinch of cayenne pepper and a few drops of liquid vegetable stock.

Sesame Seeds and Parsley
- 3 tbsp toasted sesame seeds, 3 tbsp chopped parsley and a few drops of liquid vegetable stock.

Rosemary and Garlic
- 6–8 rosemary leaves, finely chopped, ¼ tsp garlic paste and a few drops of liquid vegetable stock.

Tarragon and Tomato
- 3 tbsp chopped tarragon leaves, 2 tbsp passata (sieved tomatoes), pinch of cayenne pepper and a few drops of liquid vegetable stock.

Sweet Versions

To the yogurt, double (heavy) cream or English custard, add one of the following selections:

Coffee and Hazelnut
- 2 tbsp espresso coffee and 1 tbsp hazelnut syrup.

Raspberries and Mint
- A large handful of raspberries, crushed and 6 torn mint leaves.

Peach and Vermouth
- 2 tbsp dry vermouth and 2 ripe peaches, stones (pits) removed and chopped.

Apple and Cinnamon
- 4 tbsp apple purée and a ¼ tsp ground cinnamon.

Extra Toppings

Scatter over pancakes or waffles, with or without ice cream and syrup (pancake syrup):

- Toasted coconut mixed with finely chopped ready-to-eat dried apricots or pineapple
- Broken meringues mixed with a little ground cinnamon
- Finely chopped fudge or nougat
- Chocolate chips
- Chopped toasted nuts
- Crushed biscuits (cookies)
- Crushed butterscotch or boiled sweets
- Sliced fresh fruits

8
Not Exactly Pancakes

T IME FOR A CHANGE? You can deploy your pancake-making skills in several different ways, using the same or similar ingredients, to acquire a whole new repertoire of sweet and savoury treats.

In this chapter you will find recipes for Welsh cakes and English muffins, scones of various types, flatbreads and chapatis, all very adaptable and likely to become firm favourites. You can have some fun, and be as creative as you like, with the random mini-pancake shapes. The drop scones are a more solid version of the lighter and lacier texture you get with a crêpe, and the orange-flavoured crumpets have a really zesty appeal.

You can use a crêpe maker, a frying pan or a flat griddle for each of these recipes.

Cheese and Onion Drop Scones

Rather like small deep pancakes and very tasty. Best made and eaten warm the same day.

Makes about 18–20

1 small spring onion (scallion)
55 g / 2 oz hard cheese such as Cheddar or Red Leicester
115 g / 4 oz / 1 cup self-raising (self-rising) flour
115 g / 4 oz / 1 cup self-raising wholemeal (self-rising whole-wheat)
    flour
½ tsp prepared mustard
Pinch of freshly milled salt and black pepper
2 medium eggs
300 ml / ½ pint / 1¼ cups milk
Oil or melted butter

1. Finely chop the spring onion (scallion) and finely grate the cheese.
2. Sift the flours into a bowl and stir in the chopped spring onion (scallion), grated cheese, mustard, salt and pepper. Make a well in the centre and break in the eggs. With a wooden spoon, gently stir the flour mixture into the eggs, gradually adding the milk and mixing to make a thick batter.
3. Lightly brush the crêpe maker or a non-stick frying pan with a little oil or melted butter. Preheat the crêpe maker to 'Medium', or put the non-stick frying pan over a medium heat.
4. When hot, pour spoonfuls of batter onto the hot surface and cook until bubbles begin to rise to the surface and burst. Using a flat spatula or palette knife carefully turn the scones over and cook until golden brown on both sides.
5. Keep the drop scones warm whilst further batches are cooked.

Chapatis

The dough improves if left overnight and the chapatis will be lighter. Serve with hot spicy food, chutneys and dips.

Makes 12

225 g / 8 oz / 2 cups wholemeal (whole-wheat) flour
½ tsp salt
1 tbsp vegetable oil
Extra flour for rolling

1. Put the flour into a bowl and stir in the salt. Make a well in the centre and pour in the oil. Using your hand, gradually mix the flour into the oil and slowly add about 150 ml / ¼ pint / ²/₃ cup of water to give a firm dough.
2. Turn the dough onto a lightly floured surface and knead for 10 minutes. Wrap the dough in clear film (plastic wrap) and chill for an hour or overnight.
3. On a lightly floured surface, divide the dough into 12 portions and shape into balls. Roll each piece to a thin round like a pancake.
4. Preheat the crêpe maker or a non-stick frying pan to a hot heat (without any fat).
5. Put a chapati onto the hot surface. Cook for about 1 minute on one side until the underside is golden brown and the surface is starting to bubble. Using a flat spatula or palette knife, carefully flip the chapati over and cook the second side for about 40 seconds gently pressing the edges down with the spatula.
6. Use a clean tea towel to wrap the chapatis in as each one is cooked. Serve warm.

Parsley Potato Scones

Choose floury potatoes for best results. Serve as part of breakfast or brunch, or as an accompaniment to grilled meat or fish. I often make another version using half the quantity of potatoes mixed with the same weight of courgettes (zucchini), grated, cooked and then pressed dry.

Makes about 8–10

175 g / 6 oz cooked potato
2 tsp chopped parsley
Pinch of cayenne pepper
¼ tsp fine sea salt
2 tbsp softened butter
55 g / 2 oz / ½ cup self raising (self rising) flour, plus extra for rolling
Oil or melted butter

1. Put the potato into a bowl and finely mash.
2. Add the chopped parsley, cayenne pepper, sea salt and softened butter.
3. Mix in enough of the flour to give a stiff dough.
4. Turn the dough onto a lightly floured surface and gently knead until smooth. Roll out to a thickness of about 1 cm / ½ inch. Cut out rounds with a 6 cm / 2½ inch floured cutter. Re-roll the trimmings.
5. Lightly brush the crêpe maker or a non-stick frying pan with a little oil or melted butter. Preheat the crêpe maker to 'Medium', or put the non-stick frying pan over a medium heat.
6. Cook the scones for 3–5 minutes on each side until golden brown and cooked through.

Flatbreads

These yeasted flatbreads look rather like nan breads. Make a batch and freeze the excess. Reheat in a hot oven and, when hot, brush with garlic or chilli oil. Add flavourings into the bread mix – 1 tsp dried mixed herbs or oregano, 1 tsp garlic or chilli paste.

Makes about 18–20, depending on the packet size

1 pizza mix or white bread mix
Flour, for kneading
Oil or melted butter

1. Make up the pizza or bread dough following the packet instructions. Put into a bowl and cover with oiled clear film (plastic wrap). Leave in a warm place until doubled in size, about 45 minutes.
2. Turn the dough onto a lightly floured surface and knead until smooth.
3. Tear off pieces of dough about the size of a plum and roll each one quite thinly into ovals, teardrops or rounds. For larger flat breads, use pieces of dough about the size of a small satsuma.
4. Cover the dough shapes with oiled clear film (plastic wrap) and leave to rise for 10 minutes.
5. Lightly brush the crêpe maker or a non-stick frying pan with a little oil or melted butter. Preheat the crêpe maker to 'Medium', or put the non-stick frying pan over a medium heat.
6. Put the dough shapes onto the hot surface. Cook for about 1–3 minutes on each side until slightly blistered and just starting to brown.
7. Use a clean tea towel to wrap the flatbreads in as each one is cooked. Serve warm.

Mini Pancake Shapes

Great fun for everyone. Pour the batter from a jug or a water bottle, something to give you a little more control over the 'pour' – there are even 'pancake pourers' available in some kitchen shops. Serve with savoury dips or, while hot, sprinkle with caster sugar and serve with maple syrup or fresh fruit.

Makes plenty so freeze any excess

55 g / 2 oz / ½ cup plain (all-purpose) flour
55 g / 2 oz / ½ cup wholemeal (whole-wheat) flour
Pinch of salt
2 medium eggs
2 tbsp melted butter
300 ml / ½ pint / 1¼ cups milk
Oil or melted butter

1. Sift the flours into a bowl and add the salt. Make a well in the centre, break in the eggs and pour in the melted butter. With a whisk, gently stir the flour into the eggs, gradually adding the milk to make a smooth batter the consistency of single (light) cream. If time allows, cover and leave to stand for about 15 minutes.
2. Pour the batter into a jug.
3. Lightly brush the crêpe maker or a non-stick frying pan with a little oil or melted butter. Preheat the crêpe maker to 'Medium', or put the non-stick frying pan over a medium heat.
4. When hot, pour or drizzle small amounts of the batter to make small shapes, such as: alphabet letters, numbers, squiggles, zigzags or flower shapes. Cook gently for about 15–30 seconds (depending on their size) on one side until the underside is golden brown. Using a flat spatula or palette knife, carefully flip the shapes over and cook the second side for about 10–15 seconds. Lift out and keep warm.
5. Keep the batter-shapes warm whilst further batches are cooked.

English Muffins

English muffins are bread-like rather than cake-like. Cooked on a griddle, like bread they are then toasted. A traditional way to toast a muffin is to cut the muffin open, then close again and toast until hot all the way through. Pull open and butter the two halves.

Makes about 10–12

200 g / 7 oz / scant 1¾ cups strong white bread flour, plus extra for
  rolling
½ tsp salt
25 g / 1 oz / 2 tbsp soft butter
1 tsp fast-action dried yeast
1 medium egg
225 ml / 8 fl oz / about 1 cup milk
1 tsp semolina
Oil or melted butter

1. Sift the flour and salt into a bowl and rub in the butter until like fine crumbs. Stir in the fast-action dried yeast. Break in the egg and pour in the milk.
2. Mix to a smooth dough. Cover the bowl with oiled clear film (plastic wrap) and leave in a warm place until doubled in size, about 45 minutes to an hour.
3. Turn the dough onto a lightly floured surface and knead until smooth. Roll out to a thickness of about 1 cm / ½ inch. Cut out rounds with a

plain 7.5 cm / 3 inch floured cutter. Re-roll the trimmings.

4. Put the shapes onto a floured tray. Mix the semolina and 1 tsp flour together and sprinkle over the muffins. Cover with a cloth. Leave in a warm place until risen, about 40 minutes.

5. Lightly brush the crêpe maker or a non-stick frying pan with a little oil or melted butter. Preheat the crêpe maker to 'Medium', or put the non-stick frying pan over a medium heat.

6. Cook some of the muffins for 3–4 minutes on each side until pale golden brown and cooked through, then cook the remaining muffins.

Orange Crumpets

To give some depth, crumpets are cooked in 8 cm / 3¼ inch round metal crumpet, pastry or biscuit (cookie) cutters. If none is available, just drop spoonfuls of the mixture onto the hot surface. They will be much thinner, and more like pikelets, but just as delicious toasted and served with conserve and butter.

Makes about 10–12

175 g / 6 oz / 1½ cups strong white bread flour
¼ tsp sugar
¼ tsp salt
1¾ tsp fast-action dried yeast
100 ml / 3½ fl oz / scant ½ cup milk
Pinch of bicarbonate of soda
2 tsp grated orange rind
Oil or melted butter

1. Pour 150 ml / ¼ pint / ⅔ cup tepid water into a jug. Sift the flour, sugar and salt into a bowl and stir in the fast-action dried yeast. Stir in the milk and water and mix to a thick smooth batter. Cover the bowl with oiled clear film (plastic wrap) and leave in a warm place until doubled in size, about 45 minutes.
2. Dissolve the bicarbonate of soda in a tablespoon of water and stir with the grated orange rind into the batter. Cover and leave to rise for 15–20 minutes.
3. Lightly brush the crêpe maker or a non-stick frying pan with a little oil or melted butter. Preheat the crêpe maker to 'Medium', or put the non-stick frying pan over a medium heat.

4. Grease the metal rings and put them onto the hot surface to warm for a few seconds. Pour a spoonful of batter into each ring (about 1 cm / ½ inch deep). Cook for 3–5 minutes, depending on the depth, until bubbles begin to rise to the surface and burst. When the surface has set, remove the rings (use oven gloves) and use a flat spatula or palette knife to turn the crumpets over. Cook until a pale golden colour on both sides.

5. Make further batches and grease the metal rings each time they are used.

6. To eat them straight from the pan, cook until golden brown on both sides, otherwise toast them.

Corn Fritters

Using both sweetcorn and cornmeal adds flavour to the fritters. If cornmeal isn't available, just increase the flour.

Makes about 8

140 g / 5 oz cooked sweetcorn
2 medium eggs, separated
2 tbsp cornmeal
3 tbsp plain (all-purpose) flour
Freshly milled salt and pepper
Oil or melted butter

1. Put the sweetcorn into a bowl and stir in the egg yolks, cornmeal, flour and a little seasoning.
2. In a grease-free bowl, whisk the egg whites until they form soft peaks, then carefully fold into the corn mixture.
3. Lightly brush the crêpe maker or a non-stick frying pan with a little oil or melted butter. Preheat the crêpe maker to 'Medium', or put the non-stick frying pan over a medium heat.
4. When hot, drop spoonfuls of the mixture onto the hot surface and cook for 2–3 minutes on each side until golden brown and cooked through.
5. Keep the fritters warm while further batches are cooked.

Apricot and Walnut Griddle Scones

Best made and eaten the same day. If preferred, make with 55 g / 2 oz dried fruit in place of the apricot.

Makes about 18–20

6 ready-to-eat apricots
6 walnut halves
225 g / 8 oz / 2 cups self-raising (self-rising) flour
2 tbsp caster sugar
2 medium eggs
300 ml / ½ pint / 1¼ cups milk
Oil or melted butter

1. Finely chop the apricots and walnut halves.
2. Sift the flour into a bowl and stir in the sugar, chopped apricots and walnuts. Make a well in the centre and break in the eggs. With a wooden spoon, gently stir the flour into the eggs, gradually adding the milk and mixing to make a thick batter.
3. Lightly brush the crêpe maker or a non-stick frying pan with a little oil or melted butter. Preheat the crêpe maker to 'Medium', or put the non-stick frying pan over a medium heat.
4. When hot, pour spoonfuls of batter onto the hot surface and cook until bubbles begin to rise to the surface and burst. Using a flat spatula or palette knife, carefully turn the scones over and cook until golden brown on both sides. Lift out and keep warm.
5. Keep the drop scones warm whilst further batches are cooked.

Welsh Cakes

It's traditional to make these cakes with currants, but they're delicious, too, made with chopped, ready-to-eat dried apricots or glacé cherries. Cooked on the hob in a griddle pan or a heavy-based frying pan, these cakes freeze well.

Makes about 12

225 g / 8 oz / 2 cups self raising (self rising) flour, plus extra for rolling
2 tsp ground mixed spice
Pinch of salt
115 g / 4 oz / ½ cup butter
2 tbsp caster sugar, plus extra
85 g / 3 oz currants
2 medium eggs
A little milk
Oil or melted butter

1. Sift the flour, mixed spice and salt into a bowl. Cut the butter into small cubes and add to the flour mixture. Using your fingertips, rub the butter into the mixture until like fine crumbs. Stir in the sugar and currants.
2. Make a well in the centre and break in the eggs. Mix with a wooden spoon or palette knife, adding sufficient milk to give a soft dough.
3. Turn the dough onto a lightly floured surface and roll out to a thickness of about 1 cm / ½ inch. Cut out rounds with a 6 cm / 2½ inch floured cutter. Re-roll the trimmings.

4. Lightly brush the crêpe maker or a non-stick frying pan with a little oil or melted butter. Preheat the crêpe maker to 'Medium', or put the non-stick frying pan over a medium heat.
5. Cook the scones for 3–5 minutes on each side until golden brown and cooked through.
6. Transfer to a wire rack. While hot, sprinkle with extra caster sugar and serve warm or cold.

Index